THE PRINCETON REVIEW

Math
Smart II

BY MARCIA LERNER

Random House, Inc.
New York 1998
http://www.randomhouse.com

Princeton Review Publishing, L.L.C.
2315 Broadway
New York, NY 10024
E-mail: info@review.com

ISBN 0-679-78383-0

Edited by: Rachel Warren
Designed by: Illeny Maaza
Illustrations by: Adam Hurwitz and The Production Department of The Princeton Review
Production Editor: Amy Bryant

Manufactured in the United States of America on recycled paper.

9 8 7 6 5 4 3

First Edition

ACKNOWLEDGMENTS

Many a deeply-felt thank you to Jeannie, Melanie, Evan, and John for giving me this book, Gabriel Brownstein for great ideas and encouragement, Brendan Moran for support, Math Level II know-how, and confidence, Liz Buffa for telephone support, Rose Thomson for calming me down, Rachel Warren for scrupulous editing, and the endless efforts of Illeny Maza, Patricia Acero, Greta Englert, Jose Freire, Evelyn O'Hara, Adam Hurwitz, Robert McCormack, Carmine Raspaolo, Matt Reilly, Len Small, and Mabel Villanueva.

CONTENTS

A Brief Forward

How do you know if this book is for you? Well, this book was written to help anyone who is rusty, less than confident, or outright terrified when it comes to math. It covers high school algebra, geometry, and trigonometry; their overall usefulness, and how they work. Lots of people have had all sorts of terrible experiences with math, experiences that have left nasty tastes in their mouths. We're here to tell you that math doesn't have to be awful; it can actually be fun, rewarding, and terrifically helpful. You can certainly understand it if you try to relax as much as possible and give yourself the time. If a particular subject is proving to be frustrating, don't stay there feeling worse and worse and more confused. Take a break: Take a walk around the block, have a cookie; once you've loosened up, then you can go get a fresh piece of paper and a pencil, and start back at the beginning. If you have patience with yourself, the idea will become clear. Really.

Do I Need Preparation?

As you go through this book, you may find that some of the more basic mathematical operations are not explained. That's because we couldn't fit all of mathematics in one book if we were going to explain everything with the depth and clarity we wanted. For you to truly benefit from this book, you must first be comfortable with the following: properties of integers, properties of fractions, properties of decimals, arithmetic of integers, arithmetic of fractions and decimals, ratios and proportions, and basic geometric shapes. If any of this stuff seems foreign to you, go back and review a more basic math book. May we modestly suggest the fabulous Math Smart?

You may find, on the other hand, that you are already familiar with some of the topics you come across in this book. If this is the case, do the exercises on that topic (if there are any) to make sure you have that particular idea under control. Then move on to the next section.

WHAT DOES THIS BOOK COVER?

The basic curriculum for high school math is included here, though high schools can sometimes vary their requirements. All the math that you might encounter on the Math Level I Scholastic Assessment Test II is here, as well as much, but not all, that is on the Math Level II. If you are in an Advanced Placement course you would do well to get another book, as this book does not cover calculus, derivatives, or three-dimensional analytic geometry.

HOW DOES IT COVER THIS STUFF?

The chapters proceed through algebra, geometry, and trigonometry in roughly the order in which they are taught in most schools. Sections within these chapters are followed by exercises in which you can use your new-found knowledge to strengthen your problem-solving techniques. At the end of the book there's a glossary so that you can look up any terms you don't know.

HOW WILL THIS BOOK AFFECT YOU?

Math can be so great; it can help your mind get in shape to understand all sorts of things, and there's nothing as wonderful as the moment that you comprehend a problem that's been resisting you. You may not end up being a math-lover by the time you reach the end of this book, but you can certainly become a person for whom math is not a problem.

That said, for this book to be as helpful to you as it has the potential to be, you must actively participate in it. That means really reading through the explanations until you understand them, following along on the examples with paper and a pencil, and doing all of the exercises, and then working through the mistakes you make with the answer keys.

With that admonition in mind, you're ready to begin. Concentrate, most of all, on understanding the ideas. And have a great time.

Algebra

Well, you're heading into algebra, the subject that brings you x, y, and other mysteries. People have maligned this particular branch of mathematics over many centuries, so if it soothes you to say bad things about it don't hold back—you aren't alone. Bear in mind, though, that algebra can be extremely useful when you're working through other, larger mathematical problems and concepts. What we'll try to do first is understand what algebra is and what it does. Next we'll get comfortable with it, and then we'll move on to bigger and better things. After all, you might not enjoy learning French grammar, but when you go to France and can ask for pastries it becomes worthwhile.

To begin, you might want to know: What is algebra, anyway? Algebra is a branch of mathematics that uses letters in place of numbers. The numbers which are represented by letters in algebra are real numbers. **Real numbers** include all positive and negative integers and fractions—regular and decimal fractions. Real numbers also include roots, such as $\sqrt{5}$. Forward, now, to use this stuff.

CHAPTER 1

Algebraic Expressions

THE BASICS

A letter that stands in place of a number is called a **variable**. Why variable? Well, the letter's value varies, meaning that the numerical value which it represents is unspecified. For instance, unless a particular mathematical situation tells you differently, x has no specific numerical value. Variables are also referred to as unknowns; they can hold the place of an unknown value within an equation (a very useful function). Variables are italicized, and they can be any letter in the alphabet, though people are generally fond of a, b, c and x, y, z. And while the value of a variable is variable—heh, heh—in any one expression the value can't change. For instance, if you see something like $-a = a^2$, both a's represent the same value, whatever that value may be (do you know it?).

An **algebraic term** is a variable, a number, or a variable and a number combined by either multiplication or division. For instance, $3x$ is a term, $\frac{a}{2}$ is a term, 5 is a term, and x is a term. But $3 + y$ is two terms because the number and the variable aren't combined by multiplication or division, but by addition. A term such as $3x$, in which a variable is multiplied by a number, introduces even more vocabulary: The number 3 is a **coefficient**. The coefficient is the number by which the variable is multiplied. And when terms are combined by addition or subtraction, that combination is called an **algebraic expression.**

Algebraic expressions are more or less the first sentences you are going to speak in your new language. An algebraic expression consists of algebraic terms combined by addition or subtraction. Thus $3x - 4$ is an algebraic expression, as are $x - y$, and $\frac{4}{x} - \frac{x}{4}$. An expression put in terms of a particular variable is said to be in the terms of that variable. For instance the following algebraic expression is an expression in x.

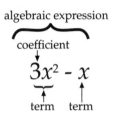

EXERCISE 1.1

1. The expression $3x - 5y$ contains how many terms?

2. The expression $3x - 5y$ contains how many variables?

3. What is the coefficient of x in the expression $3x - 5y$?

4. The number 5 is the coefficient of what variable in the expression $3x - 5y$?

5. How many terms are in the expression $3xy$?

6. In the expression $5z + 2$, what is the coefficient of z?

7. How many terms are in the expression $5z + 2$?

8. Is $4x - 4$ an algebraic expression?

SPEAKING ALGEBRA

Algebraic expressions, by the way, are the key to solving those pesky word problems of your past. Word problems require you to translate verbal sentences into math language, and beginning algebra mostly involves showing you how to do this. To advance in algebra you must be comfortable with beginning algebra, so take a moment here to review these sorts of translations.

TRANSLATING INTO MATH

To translate you must be aware of the general mathematical meanings of words. Read through the following chart until it feels familiar.

Mathematical Word	What It Means	Mathematical Sign	An Example
Product	result of multiplication	×	the product of 3 and 5, 3×5
Quotient	result of division	÷	the quotient of 4 and 2, $4 \div 2$
Difference	result of subtraction	−	the difference between 6 and 4, $6 - 4$
Sum	result of addition	+	the sum of 5 and 4, $5 + 4$
Less	minus	−	seven less three, $7 - 3$
More	plus	+	three more than two, $2 + 3$
Of	times	×	one half of six, $\frac{1}{2} \times 6$
Is	equals	=	two plus one is three, $2 + 1 = 3$
A certain number	an unknown, a variable	x (or any other variable)	a certain number less two, $x - 2$
That number	a variable or unknown previously referred to	x (or any other variable)	A certain number less two is twice that number, $x - 2 = 2x$
What	an unknown, a variable	x (or any other variable)	What less three is five? $x - 3 = 5$

These definitions make it possible for you to transcribe a verbal sentence into a mathematical expression. Thus, a verbal sentence might say *Five less than the product of a certain number and 7*. To translate this, go step by step through the pieces. *Five less than*, means subtract 5, and *the product of a certain number and 7*, means that the 5 was subtracted from the product of a variable multiplied by 7. Thus, the whole thing is written mathematically as $7x - 5$.

Example

Try translating *Four more than a certain number times 2 is one third of that number.*

Go step by step. You know that *four more than* means plus 4, and *a certain number times two* is a variable, or x times 2, which is $2x$. You have $2x + 4$. Now, try *is one third of that number.* The word *is* means equals, the *one third of* means one-third times, and the *that number* refers to the previously mentioned *a certain number*, or the variable. Write it out: $= \frac{1}{3}x$. Your complete translation is: $2x + 4 = \frac{1}{3}x$. And that's what the sentence looks like written algebraically.

EXERCISE 1.2

Try a few exercises in translation on your own.

1. The product of a certain number and ten, less six.

2. Three more than the quotient of a certain number and two.

3. Two less than a certain number.

4. Five-sixths of a certain number, less one, is half that number.

Try writing the next of these out verbally.

5. $\frac{x}{2} + 17$

6. $12 + 9x$

7. $\frac{w}{4} + 5$

8. $\frac{t}{2} - 6$

FORMULAS

People also use algebraic expressions to express fixed relationships. These fixed relationships are called **formulas.** You are probably familiar with the old $E = mc^2$ from Einstein or the beginning credits of *The Twilight Zone.* Don't worry, we won't explain $E = mc^2$ here; it's just an example of a formula. Formulas use particular variables to express their components; these variables are usually defined below the formula. A formula will generally be presented in this way:

$$E = mc^2$$

in which E stands for energy, m for mass, and c for the speed of light.

Formulas and other algebraic expressions can also contain algebraic terms called **constants.** A constant term has a fixed numerical value within an expression or series of expressions. For example, in the formula $E = mc^2$, c has a constant value, not a variable one; it always represents 299,792,460 miles per second—the speed of light.

EVALUATING AN EXPRESSION

Formulas are sometimes followed by specific values to be put into the formula. A question might look like this:

$$A = \frac{1}{2} bh$$

in which A is the area of a triangle with base b and height h. What is the area of a triangle with a base of 4 and a height of 6?

All you do in a case like this is substitute in the values given for the variables and solve it as though it were an arithmetic problem.

$$A = \frac{1}{2}(4)(6) \text{ becomes } A = \frac{1}{2}(24) \text{ becomes } A = 12$$

Solving for specific values as we just did is called **evaluating a formula.** It is one of the basic jobs of the algebra student. What else do they ask you to do with formulas? You may be asked to translate verbal statements into formulas. This, of course, you are well-prepared for from previous translation, so try it on the next exercise.

EXERCISE 1.3

Translate the following sentences into formulas, using whichever variables you think are appropriate: For instance, the first initial of a word always makes a nice variable.

1. The distance traveled is equivalent to the rate of speed times the time taken.

2. The volume of a rectangular solid is equal to the length times the width times the height.

3. A person's height is equal to the width of her arms from the tip of her middle finger to the tip of her middle finger.

4. The circumference of a circle is equal to π times its diameter.

Now, evaluate the following formulas.

5. $D = T \times R$
in which D represents distance traveled, T represents time and R represents rate of travel. How far has a car traveled if it goes for 2 hours at the rate of 60 miles per hour?

6. $v = l \times w \times h$
in which v represents the volume of a rectangular solid and l, w, and h are its length, width, and height respectively. What is the volume of a rectangular solid of length 3, width 5, and height 2?

7. $h = a$
in which h is a person's height and a is the width of his arms spread. How tall is a person if the width of his arms is 64″?

8. $c = \pi d$
in which c is the circumference of a circle and d is the diameter. What is the circumference of a circle of diameter 12?

PARENTHESES

There are various symbols within expressions that affect their meaning. **Parentheses** are used to group parts of expressions and make the orders of various mathematical operations more clear. Parentheses are particularly useful when you're dealing with variables, as you are in algebra. For instance, the expression $a - b$ is always only $a - b$; we can't simplify it further. If that amount is to be added to another amount, parentheses are used to point out that the entire $(a - b)$ is being added.

Parentheses can also be used to denote multiplication, either with actual numbers or with variables. For instance, $5(6)$ is 5×6, and $a(b)$ is $a \times b$, which can also be expressed as ab or $a \cdot b$.

Brackets { } and **braces** or **fences** [ ] are simply variations of parentheses, and are used in cases where there are quantities within quantities, in this order: $\{[()]\}$. For instance, $c\{a - b[x - y(z + w)]\}$ expresses a whole chain of operations and even tells you in which order to perform them. The overall **order of operations** for any expression, mathematical or algebraic, is Parentheses-Exponents-Multiplication-Division-Addition-Subtraction, also known by its initials as **PEMDAS**. The multiplication and division in that chain are interchangeable with respect to order and the addition and subtraction operations go left to right as they are written in the expression. With parentheses, do the innermost set first and work your way out.

Example

What is $2\{3 + [8 - 5(-6 \div -2) + 7] - 2\}$?

Start at the inside and work your way out. The innermost set of parentheses here contains –6 divided by –2. Perform that division.

$$2\{3 + [8 - 5(3) + 7] - 2\}$$

Next is multiplication within the braces. That means the 5 times the 3; once that product is found, the addition and subtraction can be performed left to right.

$$2\{3 + [8 - 15 + 7] - 2\} \text{ becomes } 2\{3 + [0] - 2\}$$

Again, the brackets go first, so add what is within them.

$$2\{1\}$$

Now you can multiply, and your answer is 2. Now you're a champion of the world of parentheses.

If you're entirely unfamiliar with the order of operations (PEMDAS), go back to *Math Smart* or any other basic math book and review. And don't worry, generally you won't have to translate long, involved expressions of this sort; all you'll have to do is understand them. To help with this, read on.

THE LAW

You've probably encountered any number of laws over your early math years and thought, "What could possibly be the point of learning this? I'll forget it immediately." Well, the laws have stubbornly returned to show you that they do have good reasons for existing, you were wrong to spurn them, but if you'll just take a minute and review them all will be forgiven.

The first of these is the **commutative law**. This law states that any single operation is the same no matter what its order is; there is a commutative law of addition and a commutative law of multiplication. Essentially these laws mean that $a + b$ is the same as $b + a$, and that $a \times b$ is the same as $b \times a$. Pretty clear, and look—you just read some algebra.

The second of these laws is the **associative law**. This law states that no matter which way an operation is grouped its result remains the same. Again, there is an associative law of addition and an associative law of multiplication. This means that $a + (b + c)$ is the same as $(a + b) + c$ which is the same as $(a + c) + b$. For multiplication it means that $a \times (b \times c)$ is the same as $(a \times b) \times c$ which is the same as $(a \times c) \times b$.

Along with those laws is the law that is most important in understanding and working with algebraic expressions: the **distributive law**. The distributive law shows that multiplying by a combined sum is the same as multiplying by each part of the sum and then adding those multiplied parts.

In algebraic terms: $a \times (b + c)$ is the same as $(a \times b) + (a \times c)$.

This works with subtracting as well; multiplying by the result of a subtraction is the same as multiplying by each part of the subtraction and then subtracting those multiplied parts.

So: $a \times (b - c)$ is the same as $(a \times b) - (a \times c)$.

This is one fantastic law, and it will help you in both the arithmetic and algebraic worlds. Arithmetically, it allows you to perform large number multiplications much more easily. For instance, if someone were to come running up to you gasping, "Quick! If I can find the answer to 99 times 5, I win a free trip to Rio!" You can smoothly think to yourself, "Why, 99 times 5 is really 100 times 5 minus 1 times 5, or 500 minus 5, or 495." Then you can tell the person or not, depending on how benevolent you're feeling and whether they might take you along.

$$99 \times 5 = (100 \times 5) - (1 \times 5) = 500 - 5 = 495$$

You can also use the distributive law to expand or contract various algebraic expressions. For instance to expand $3m(n + q - r)$ you could use the distributive law to rewrite it like so: $3mn + 3mq - 3mr$. Notice that all you're doing is what the distributive law tells you *can* do, which is multiply each term inside the parentheses by the outer term, and then perform the appropriate operation; addition or subtraction. To contract expressions by using the distributive law, go in the other direction. Instead of moving from $a(b + c)$ to $ab + ac$, move from $ab + ac$ to $a(b + c)$. In order to do this, we first need to find a factor that is common to both terms in the expression. In this case the common factor is a, (it's present in both terms). Common factors can be variables, numbers, or a combination of both of these.

Take a look at this expression and try to find the common factor: $2x^2 + 4x$. What is the common factor of the two terms? Well, $2x$ looks good to us, because both terms have 2 as well as x as common factors. Practice will help a lot in finding factors, as will going step by step. If you didn't see that right away, don't despair. Dividing the $2x$ out of the expression gives you $2x(x + 2)$. To check your work, multiply according to the distributive law; it comes out beautifully.

Example

Factor: $ab^2c - a^2bc - abc^2$

First, what are the common factors of the three terms? Both have at least abc, do they have any more? No. Divide out abc from each term and put it outside the parentheses. You get $abc(b - a - c)$, so that is the factored form of the expression.

SIMPLIFYING BY COMBINING LIKE TERMS

If you came upon the expression $ac + ab + 3ac$, how could you simplify it? Well, you could certainly factor out the a. And you could combine like terms. What are like terms? They are terms that share the same variables or don't have any variables at all. Above, ac and $3ac$ are like terms. Sure, one of them has a coefficient of 3, but that just means you have three groups of ac, you could combine them with the other ac to get $4ac$, or four groups of ac. If you had factored the expression, you would have $a(c + b + 3c)$ and you could combine like terms c and $3c$ to get $a(b + 4c)$. It should be noted that if terms have exponents, in order to be like terms they must have the same exponent. For instance, $3x$ and $4x$ are like terms, $4x^2$ and x^2 are like terms, but $4x^2$ and $3x$ are NOT like terms because their variables have different exponents. More will be said on the reason that unlike exponents can't be combined in the next section, where you will find out everything you ever wanted to know about exponents.

To combine like terms, simply add or subtract as indicated. So the terms $3x + 4x$ become $7x$, and the terms $4x^2 - x^2$ become $3x^2$. (No visible coefficient indicates a coefficient of one.)

EXERCISE 1.4

1. Solve: 13×20
2. Solve: 42×101
3. Expand: $a(c + d)$
4. Simplify: $(2x - y) - [x - (x + y)]$
5. Simplify: $x + \{2x - y[x + 2y - (3x + 2y)]\}$

6. Factor: $ax^2 + bx - cx$

7. Factor: $3x^2 - 12x + 9$

8. Factor: $\dfrac{4}{x} - \dfrac{2}{x^2}$

ANSWERS TO CHAPTER ONE EXERCISES

ANSWERS TO EXERCISE 1.1

1. Two terms, $3x$ and $5y$

2. Two variables, x and y

3. 3 is the coefficient of x

4. 5 is the coefficient of y

5. One term

6. 5 is the coefficient of z

7. Two terms, $5z$ and 2

8. Yup

ANSWERS TO EXERCISE 1.2

1. $10x - 6$

2. $\dfrac{x}{2} + 3$

3. $x - 2$

4. $\dfrac{5}{6}x - 1 = \dfrac{x}{2}$

   Note: The following represent just one possible translation; you may have used slightly different wording. Make sure that you've got the expressions you want by translating from your sentences back to algebra.

5. Seventeen more than one-half of a certain number.

6. Twelve increased by the product of a certain number and nine.

7. Five more than the quotient of w and four.

8. Six less than the product of t and one-half.

ANSWERS TO EXERCISE 1.3

1. $D = R \times T$
2. $v = l \times w \times h$
3. $h = w$
4. $c = \pi d$
5. distance $= 120$ miles
6. volume $= 30$
7. height $= 64$ inches or 5 feet 4 inches (same thing)
8. circumference $= 12\pi$

ANSWERS TO EXERCISE 1.4

1. 260
   The easiest way to do this is probably to split up the 13 so you are not multiplying by such an odd and awkward number. In other words, $20 \cdot 13$ (remember the commutative property?) becomes $20(10 + 3)$ which becomes $20(10) + 20(3)$ becomes $200 + 60$ or 260. You could also look at this as 13 times 10 plus 13 times 10, in another worthy strive towards the easier maneuver.

2. 4,242
   The number 101 can be split up into 100 and 1. So you get $42(100) + 42(1) = 4200 + 42 = 4,242$.

3. $ac + ad$

4. $2x$
   Take these kinds of problems slowly and carefully and you'll be all right. First tackle the innermost parentheses which are presented here in bold, $(2x - y) - [x - (x + y)]$. Since you can't simplify this expression more, the next step is to look outside it. The first thing you should notice is the subtraction sign that indicates that the entire expression $(x + y)$ is to be subtracted from the x; $(2x - y) - [x - (x + y)]$. The x's disappear when subtracted, and you are left with $-y$. $(2x - y) - [-y]$. You can now subtract the whole thing, as there are no multiplication signs or layers of parentheses. The two subtraction signs present the y as being added to the $-y$ in the first set, the y's disappear, and you are left with $2x$.

5. $3x + 2xy$

For a convoluted expression such as this one, start with the innermost set of parentheses and work your way outward. In this case, the innermost set is the $(3x + 2y)$ with which you can do nothing by itself, so go directly outside it. You see it is subtracted from $x + 2y$. Thus, subtract: $x + 2y - (3x + 2y)$. The $3x$ subtracts from x giving $-2x$, and $2y$ subtracts from the $2y$, leaving nothing. You're left with the overall expression of $x + \left\{2x - y[-2x]\right\}$. Now you can multiply by the y outside the innermost bracket to get $x + \left\{2x - (-2xy)\right\}$, which becomes $x + \{2x + 2xy\}$ due to the two negative signs. You can then add, regardless of the brackets, due to the associative law of addition, and get $3x + 2xy$. Whew.

6. $x(ax + b - c)$

7. $3(x^2 - 4x + 3)$

8. $\dfrac{2}{x}\left(2 - \dfrac{1}{x}\right)$

The factor here is a fraction, and we'll bet that didn't faze you a bit. Divide it out of the terms, and you've got a factored expression.

CHAPTER 2

Algebraic Equations

SOLVING EQUATIONS

Now that you are comfortable with algebraic expressions and some of the laws that govern them, it's time to move on to the case of the expression that is set equal to something. An algebraic expression that is set equal to something is called an **algebraic equation**. Some examples of equations are $3x - 2y = 0$, $ax^2 + bx + c = 0$, $3x - 2 = 7$, and $4x - 1 = 16y$.

You might notice something about these equations. One of them is going to be easy to solve numerically because it contains only one variable, and the variable has no exponent. This equation—did you notice it?—is $3x - 2 = 7$. To solve an algebraic equation—one with only one variable—means to find the numerical value of the variable. To determine its value you must first **isolate** it, which means getting it alone on one side of the equation.

In cases where the equation contains more than one variable, you can solve for one variable by expressing it in terms of the other variables. For instance, you can find out what variable x equals in terms of the variable y. This also means isolating whichever variable is in question. Altogether, if you're solving numerically or only in terms of another variable, isolating a variable is something you want to get very comfortable doing.

BUT HOW DO I ISOLATE A VARIABLE?
HOW CAN SUCH A THING BE POSSIBLE?

How nice of you to ask. The reason isolating a variable is possible is that you can manipulate equations and move around their parts. The equation $3x - 2 = 7$ has two sides separated by an equals sign. To get the x alone you need to get the numbers on one side and the variable on the other. So, you must do things to this equation to move its parts. What can you do? In fact, you can do anything you want to an equation, *provided you do it to both sides of the equation.* Slow down and read that again. Maybe it should even be in a special box: It's that important.

> You can do anything you want to an equation, provided you do it to both sides of the equation.

To get the variable in $3x - 2 = 7$ alone on one side, first move the 2 to the other side. The way to move something from one side of an equation to another is to perform the opposite operation to both sides of the equation. In other words, since 2 is being subtracted from $3x$, you do the opposite; you add it, to both sides.

$$3x - 2 = 7$$
$$3x - 2 + 2 = 7 + 2$$
$$3x = 9$$

Now, to move the coefficient 3 we again do the opposite: Since the variable is being multiplied by 3, we divide both sides by 3.

$$3x = 9$$
$$\frac{3x}{3} = \frac{9}{3}$$
$$x = 3$$

And voila, you have solved the equation by isolating the variable, you know that $x = 3$.

LIKE TERMS

Some equations look more imposing, for instance, $3x + 2 = 4x$. Is this an equation you can solve numerically by isolating the variable? Sure. It's still an equation with only one variable—x. Certainly the variable is in two different places, but don't let this faze you; you can take care of it because you can combine like terms. You already know how to do that, so go ahead and move the like terms to one side of the equation by subtracting $3x$ from both sides.

$$3x + 2 = 4x$$
$$3x + 2 - 3x = 4x - 3x$$
$$2 = x$$

Example

Try solving the following equation: $5x - 7 = 3x - 1$.

To isolate the variable here, you must first decide which side is a better place to gather the variables. Generally it's easier to move the variable with the smaller coefficient, but either way the solution will come out the same, so don't let worrying about it slow you down. For this demonstration, we will move the variable with the smaller coefficient—the coefficient 3 on the right side as opposed to the 5 on the left. To move the added $3x$ from the right side of the equation we must do the opposite, in other words subtract it from both sides. How did we know it was being added? Because it appears as a positive term.

$$5x - 7 = 3x - 1$$
$$5x - 7 - 3x = 3x - 1 - 3x$$
$$2x - 7 = -1$$

Once you've combined $5x$ and $3x$, move the numbers to the other side. Here, the 7 is subtracted so you need to do the opposite, add it, to both sides.

$$2x - 7 = -1$$
$$2x - 7 + 7 = -1 + 7$$
$$2x = 6$$

Now, what about the multiplied 2? Divide by 2 to move it, and divide it on both sides, because you wouldn't even think of doing anything to just one side now, would you?

$$\frac{2x}{2} = \frac{6}{2}$$
$$x = 3$$

And there is your isolated variable, $x = 3$.

SIMULTANEOUS EQUATIONS

Do you think you've seen it all? Well you haven't quite yet. You're probably fairly expert at isolating a variable in an equation, but what can you do when you have two variables?

Pairs or groups of equations that are distinct yet contain the same variables are called either **simultaneous linear equations** or **linear systems of equations**. Why are they called systems? Because they encompass a system of equations, usually two equations but sometimes more. Why are they called linear? You'll find out all about linearity soon; suffice it to say for now that a linear equation is an equation in which the variables do not have exponents.

The equations $3x + 4y = 5$ and $3x + y = 2$ can form a linear equation system; the equations $3x + 4y = 5$ and $2a + 3b = 7$ cannot, because they do not contain the same variables, thus they do not comprise a system together.

There are two ways to solve simultaneous equations: By combining the equations and by substituting. We'll look at combining the equations first, because it's cooler.

By *combining*, we mean adding or subtracting the equations to make one of the variables disappear. How do we decide whether to add or subtract? Look at the equation system and see which operation will eliminate one or the other of the variables. Two terms with exactly the same variable and coefficient will disappear if you subtract one from the other, and two terms with the same variable and coefficient except for the sign—positive or negative—will disappear when added.

For instance, in the case of the linear equation system $3x + 4y = 5$ and $3x + y = 2$, subtraction works. Stack the equations in whichever order you prefer and subtract them.

$$\begin{array}{r} 3x + 4y = 5 \\ - \ (3x + \ y = 2) \\ \hline 0 + 3y = 3 \end{array}$$

Now isolate y.

$$3y = 3 \text{ becomes } y = 1.$$

To find x now that you have y all you have to do is substitute the y back into either equation. If y is 1 and $3x + y = 2$ then $3x + 1 = 2$. You can isolate the x; $3x = 1$, $x = \dfrac{1}{3}$. To test these two values, put them into both equations. You know they work in the second equation, so try the first.

$$3(\tfrac{1}{3}) + 4(1) = 5 \text{ becomes } 1 + 4 = 5.$$

Does it look good to you? It sure looks good to us.

To decide whether adding or subtracting is appropriate, study the equation system. Which will leave you with an equation containing only one variable? That's the one to use.

Sometimes you'll find equation systems that don't have a term with the same combination of coefficient and variable, so it won't seem as though either adding or subtracting will help you. In this case you can multiply one of the equations through in order to make one of its terms the same as a term in the other equation. It's a lot like finding a common denominator.

$$2x - 5y = 6 \text{ and } 4x + y = 1$$

They don't easily add or subtract; we can multiply the second equation by 5 (or multiply the first by 2, if you'd like) and the problem becomes much clearer.

$$2x - 5y = 6 \text{ and } 20x + 5y = 5$$

Now, how do we get rid of those $5y$'s? Here, addition is the operation of choice.

$$\begin{array}{r} 2x - 5y = 6 \\ + \left(20x + 5y = 5\right) \\ \hline 22x = 11 \end{array}$$

$$x = \frac{11}{22} \text{ or } \frac{1}{2}$$

To find y, substitute the value of x back into either equation.

$$2\left(\frac{1}{2}\right) - 5y = 6$$
$$1 - 5y = 6$$
$$-5y = 5$$
$$y = -1$$

To check your work, try these values in the other equation.

SUBSTITUTING

Substituting, which is the other method for solving systems of linear equations, involves solving for one variable in terms of the other in one equation, and then substituting the expression for that variable into the other equation. We can try it on this system.

$$3x + 2y = 4$$
$$2x + y = 6$$

Certainly you could multiply through and then add or subtract, but substituting will get you the same result in a slightly different way. Solve the second equation for y.

$$y = 6 - 2x$$

Now you can substitute that value for y into the first equation. Since the first equation has $2y$, you can substitute in twice the value of y you determined from the second equation.

$$3x + 2(6 - 2x) = 4$$
$$3x + 12 - 4x = 4$$

Now you have an equation with only one variable, x. Solve it.

$$-x + 12 = 4$$
$$-x = -8$$
$$x = 8$$

To find y, substitute this value for x into either equation.

$$y = 6 - 2(8)$$
$$y = 6 - 16$$
$$y = -10$$

Check your work by making sure this pair of values works in both equations, and then you're in business.

Example

What are the values of x and y in the linear equation system $2x - 4 = y$ and $3x + y = 2$?

Either substituting or combining will work here. We'll combine first. Organize the equations so that they're in the same order and can easily be added or subtracted.

$$2x - 4 = y \text{ becomes } 2x - 4 - y = 0 \text{ becomes } 2x - y = 4$$

$$2x - y = 4$$
$$3x + y = 2$$

Which operation should we use? Well, addition will eliminate the y's, which have the same coefficient but opposite signs:

$$\begin{array}{r} 2x - y = 4 \\ + \ 3x + y = 2 \\ \hline 5x = 6 \end{array}$$

$$x = \frac{6}{5}$$

Find y by substituting the value of x back in:

$3\left(\dfrac{6}{5}\right)+y=2$ becomes $\dfrac{18}{5}+y=2$ becomes $y=2-\dfrac{18}{5}$ becomes $y=-\dfrac{8}{5}$.

To use the substitution method to solve these equations, $2x-4=y$ and $3x+y=2$, it's easiest to substitute in the value of the already isolated y from the first equation into the second equation:

$$3x + 2x - 4 = 2$$
$$5x - 4 = 2$$
$$5x = 6$$
$$x = \dfrac{6}{5}$$

Find y by substituting this value back into either equation.

Important warning: If you have two forms of the identical equation, $x + y = 3$ and $2x + 2y = 6$, for instance, finding the values of x and y is not possible through these methods; you need a system of equations, not just one equation expressed differently.

EXERCISE 2.1

Try solving the following algebraic equations for one or both variables.

1. $3x - 2 = x + 5$

2. $4a = 3 - a$

3. $2x - 3y = 5$ and $x + 3y = 7$

4. $-2a = 3a - 6$

5. $3x = 2y - 5$ and $5x + 2y = 3$

6. $6 - b = -2b - 6$

7. $4x = 5y$ and $2x - 7y = 12$

8. $-a = a + 3$

SOLVING EQUATIONS THAT CONTAIN ALGEBRAIC FRACTIONS

And what does one do when faced with an equation like this: $\frac{x}{3} + 2 = 4x$? This is an equation that contains an **algebraic fraction**. Well, algebraic fractions follow the rules of all other fractions: To add or subtract them they must have a common denominator (and remember, fractions are just expressions of division).

As for the equation $\frac{x}{3} + 2 = 4x$, there are a number of ways to go about isolating the variable, and we will show you the two most important. First you could simply subtract the variable with the smaller coefficient, in this case the term on the left side where the coefficient is $\frac{1}{3}$. It would look like this:

$$\frac{x}{3} + 2 - \frac{x}{3} = 4x - \frac{x}{3}$$

To subtract on the right side you need a common denominator, and the easiest way to get one is by using the bow tie.

THE BOW TIE

The bow tie is an easy way to find a common denominator.

$$\frac{4x}{1} \diagdown \frac{x}{3} = \frac{11x}{3}$$
$$12(x) \quad - \quad (x)$$

Let's look at it step by step. First multiply up from the denominator of the second fraction to the numerator of the first:

$$12(x)$$
$$\frac{4x}{1} \diagdown \frac{x}{3}$$

Then multiply the denominator of the first by the numerator of the second:

$$12(x) \quad - \quad (x)$$
$$\frac{4x}{1} \diagup\diagdown \frac{x}{3}$$

Then multiply the denominators to produce the final denominator:

$$\frac{4x}{1} \bowtie \frac{x}{3} = \frac{12(x) \ - \ (x)}{3}$$

Then add or subtract the numerators as directed and you're done!

$$\frac{4x}{1} \bowtie \frac{x}{3} = \frac{12(x) \ - \ (x)}{3} = \frac{11x}{3}$$

"AS WE WERE SAYING..."

Now, back to our problem.

$$\frac{x}{3} + 2 - \frac{x}{3} = 4x - \frac{x}{3}$$

Using the bow tie on the right half of the equation makes your equation looks like this:

$$2 = \frac{11x}{3}$$

To isolate the x, do what you would normally do: perform the opposite operation from what occurs in the equation: multiply both sides by 3.

$$2 \times 3 = \frac{11x}{3} \times 3$$

$$6 = 11x$$

Finally, divide both sides by 11, and you're left with just your variable.

$$\frac{6}{11} = \frac{11x}{11} \text{ becomes } \frac{6}{11} = x$$

The other way you can isolate the variable in that problem is to get rid of the denominator of the fraction before you even begin adding or subtracting.

Here's the original equation again:

$$\frac{x}{3} + 2 = 4x$$

Instead of just subtracting $\frac{x}{3}$ from both sides, you could multiply the whole equation through by 3. The thing to remember here is that you must multiply every part of both sides, like so:

$$3\left(\frac{x}{3} + 2\right) = 3(4x)$$

Remember the distributive law here: When you multiply the left side by 3, you multiply *each term* in the left side by 3. By multiplying through,

$$3\left(\frac{x}{3} + 2\right) = 3(4x) \text{ becomes } x + 6 = 12x$$

Now, proceed to combine like terms and isolate that rascally variable.

$$x + 6 - x = 12x - x$$
$$6 = 11x$$

$$\frac{6}{11} = \frac{11x}{11} \text{ becomes } \frac{6}{11} = x$$

Same right answer, a subtly different way of getting it. And it all goes back to the wonderful distributive law, whose importance and reliability we're sure you're beginning to appreciate.

EXERCISE 2.2

Try solving a few more equations on your own.

1. $3a - 1 = 2a$

2. $6 = 7x$

3. $5 - 2a = 2a - 5$

4. $3a - 3 = -3$

5. $\frac{a}{4} + 1 = 5$

6. $2y = 3 + \frac{y}{2}$

7. $14 = -12 - \frac{2}{x}$

8. $5a = 17 - \frac{a}{2}$

A BIT MORE ABOUT ALGEBRAIC FRACTIONS

As we said earlier, fractions are merely expressions of division, a fact you are probably already long familiar with. So when you have an algebraic expression with fractions, one way to simplify it is to divide. Take this expression:

$$\frac{\frac{x}{y}}{x} + \frac{1}{y}$$

To simplify it, look at the term on the left. The x on the bottom is really $\frac{x}{1}$, so you can see that the term has two stacked fractions, the one on the top divided by the one on the bottom. Well, dividing fractions just means inverting the bottom fraction and then multiplying, like so.

$\frac{\frac{x}{y}}{x} + \frac{1}{y}$ becomes $\left(\frac{x}{y} \times \frac{1}{x}\right) + \frac{1}{y}$ which becomes, by cancellation, $\frac{1}{y} + \frac{1}{y}$.

You already have a common denominator, and you can just add.

$$\frac{1}{y} + \frac{1}{y} = \frac{2}{y}$$

And there is your expression, simplified: $\frac{\frac{x}{y}}{x} + \frac{1}{y}$ is really $\frac{2}{y}$.

Try some on your own.

EXERCISE 2.3

1. $\left(\frac{1}{x} - 1\right) + (x - 1)$

2. $\frac{3x}{y} \times \frac{1}{x}$

3. $\dfrac{2}{x - \left(\frac{1}{2} - x\right)}$

4. $\dfrac{4}{(x + 1)} - \dfrac{2}{(x - 1)}$

5. $\dfrac{(x - 1)}{2x} - \dfrac{2x}{(x - 1)}$

6. $3x + \dfrac{3}{x}$

7. $\dfrac{x}{2y} - \dfrac{2y}{x}$

8. $\dfrac{y}{(x-1)} + \dfrac{y}{(1-x)}$

ANSWERS TO CHAPTER TWO EXERCISES

ANSWERS TO EXERCISE 2.1

1. $x = 3.5$

2. $a = \dfrac{3}{5}$

3. $x = 4,\ y = 1$
   Just add them; they're simultaneous equations.

4. $a = \dfrac{6}{5}$

5. $x = -\dfrac{1}{4},\ y = \dfrac{17}{8}$

6. $b = -12$

7. $x = \dfrac{10}{3},\ y = -\dfrac{8}{3}$

8. $a = -\dfrac{3}{2}$

ANSWERS TO EXERCISE 2.2

1. $a = 1$

2. $x = \dfrac{6}{7}$

3. $a = \dfrac{5}{2}$

4. $a = 0$
   There are a million ways to solve this, and the easiest is to add 3 to both sides to get $3a = 0$, and then isolate a. But you could also factor this equation to get $3(a-1) = -3$, then divide both sides by 3 and solve it that way. It's not so much that one is easier than another, it's just that you should be aware

that there are different ways of looking at any equation, and the more you try to see these different ways, the more you *will* see, and the more comfortable with math you'll become.

5. $a = 16$

6. $y = 2$

You could approach this in a number of ways, but we'll show you the first one that occurred to us. Multiply both sides of the equation by 2. You get $4y = 6 + y$. (Why the 6? Well, the whole right side must be multiplied by 2, because of the distributive property, remember?) Now subtract y from both sides to get $3y = 6$. Then divide both sides by 3 to get $y = 2$.

7. $x = -\dfrac{1}{13}$

8. $a = \dfrac{34}{11}$

ANSWERS TO EXERCISE 2.3

1. $\dfrac{x^2 - 2x + 1}{x}$ or $\dfrac{(x - 1)^2}{x}$

Here's how to work it. First simplify the left parentheses by changing the 1 to $\dfrac{x}{x}$ and subtracting. This leaves you with $\dfrac{1 - x}{x}$. Now you want to add this to $x - 1$. The bow tie gives you $\dfrac{x^2 - x}{x}$. Now you can add; you get $\dfrac{1 - x + x^2 - x}{x}$. You can rearrange it like so: $\dfrac{x^2 - 2x + 1}{x}$. The factorization next to it will be explained in an upcoming section.

2. $\dfrac{3}{y}$

3. $\dfrac{4}{4x - 1}$

Whew, this one takes a couple of steps. First subtract the terms in the parentheses by getting the common denominator 2, and

you get $\dfrac{2}{x - \left(\dfrac{1-2x}{2}\right)}$. Then find a common denominator for the x

outside the parentheses and subtract from there to get

$\dfrac{2}{\dfrac{2x}{2} - \left(\dfrac{1-2x}{2}\right)}$, which is $\dfrac{2}{\left(\dfrac{4x\ -\ 1}{2}\right)}$, which is 2 times $\dfrac{2}{4x\ -\ 1}$,

which is $\dfrac{4}{4x\ -\ 1}$.

4. $\dfrac{2(x - 3)}{(x + 1)(x - 1)}$

Use the bow tie method to get $\dfrac{(4x-4)-(2x+2)}{(x+1)(x-1)}$ which be-

comes $\dfrac{2x-6}{(x+1)(x-1)}$. Factor out the common factor of 2 at the

top and get $\dfrac{2(x-3)}{(x+1)(x-1)}$.

5. $\dfrac{5x^2 - 2x + 1}{2x^2 - 2x}$

6. $\dfrac{3\left(x^2 + 1\right)}{x}$ or $\dfrac{3x^2 + 3}{x}$

Either of the above is okay because they both indicate the same thing.

7. $\dfrac{x^2 - 4y^2}{2xy}$

No real surprises; this is the same basic question as number five, and by now you're an old pro at handling these. Get a common denominator by using the bow tie method, and you've got yourself an answer.

8. This problem is just like any of these others. You use the bow tie to get a common denominator: $\dfrac{(y-xy)+(xy-y)}{(x-1)(1-x)}$. You combine the like terms on top and get 0, and you don't even have to multiply through. Any fraction with 0 for its numerator is equal to 0. Very nice.

CHAPTER **3**

Exponents and Roots

EXPONENTS

Now that you are fairly comfortable with algebraic notation and you know how to manipulate algebraic expressions (aren't you impressed with yourself?), it's time to add an understanding of roots and **exponents** to your algebraic arsenal. An exponent, as you may already know, is the tiny number that indicates how many of the base numbers are multiplied by each other.

$$3^{4} \longleftarrow \text{exponent}$$
$$\longleftarrow \text{base}$$

For instance, 3^4 means that you are multiplying four 3's by one another, like this: $3 \times 3 \times 3 \times 3$,

and x^5 is $x \times x \times x \times x \times x$.

The whole term, base and exponent together, is generally called a power. When the exponent is 2, it's sometimes called a *square*. When the exponent is 3, sometimes it's called a *cube*.

x^2 is x *squared*.

x^3 is x *cubed*.

As you can tell if you look at them for a moment, positive numbers raised to even or odd powers will remain positive. For instance, 3^2 is 9, 3^3 is 27, and $-\dfrac{1}{2}^3$ is $-\dfrac{1}{8}$. (Tricky how we slipped that fraction in there, wasn't it? Fractions raised to powers are multiplied by themselves top and bottom just as any other number is.) Negative numbers are a slightly different story. When you raise negative numbers to even powers, the result is positive, so -3^2 is 9. But when you raise negative numbers to odd powers, they stay negative, as you can see here: -2^3 is -8, -5^5 is -225, and $-\dfrac{1}{3}^3$ is $-\dfrac{1}{27}$. This makes perfect sense when you realize that the regular numbers you see every day are being raised to their invisible first powers, for example -5 is actually also -5^1.

RULES OF EXPONENTS

In algebra you are often called upon to add, multiply, divide, subtract, or otherwise fool around with powers. Happily there are a few simple rules that you can use to handle these situations:

Rule of Multiplication: When multiplying powers with the same base, add the exponents. $x^4 \cdot x^3 = x^7$

Why? Because $(x \cdot x \cdot x \cdot x)(x \cdot x \cdot x) = x^7$
If powers have different bases, they cannot be multiplied by adding their exponents. So $x^2 \cdot y^3 = x^2y^3$

Rule of Division: To divide powers that have the same base, subtract the exponents. $\dfrac{x^8}{x^3} = x^5$

Why? Because $\dfrac{x^8}{x^3} = \dfrac{x \cdot x \cdot x \cdot x \cdot x \cdot x \cdot x \cdot x}{x \cdot x \cdot x}$ = [now with canceling

$\dfrac{x \cdot x \cdot x \cdot x \cdot x \cdot \cancel{x} \cdot \cancel{x} \cdot \cancel{x}}{\cancel{x} \cdot \cancel{x} \cdot \cancel{x}}] = x^5$
If powers have different bases, they cannot be divided by subtracting their exponents, so $\dfrac{y^6}{x^3} = \dfrac{y^6}{x^3}$

Rules of Raising: To raise a power to another exponent, multiply the exponents. $\left(x^4\right)^2 = x^8$

Why? Because you are squaring the whole unit, so $(x \cdot x \cdot x \cdot x)$ $(x \cdot x \cdot x \cdot x) = x \cdot x \cdot x \cdot x \cdot x \cdot x \cdot x \cdot x = x^8$

Rules of Parentheses: When you raise something within parentheses to a power, every piece of the term within the parentheses is raised to that power. $(xy)^2 = x^2y^2$ and $\left(\dfrac{x}{y}\right)^3 = \dfrac{x^3}{y^3}$

Why? Well, the section on parentheses should explain most of this, but the nitty gritty is that $(xy)^2$ is $(xy)(xy) = x \cdot x \cdot y \cdot y = x^2y^2$

Also, $\left(\dfrac{x}{y}\right)^3$ is $\left(\dfrac{x}{y}\right)\left(\dfrac{x}{y}\right)\left(\dfrac{x}{y}\right) = \dfrac{x \cdot x \cdot x}{y \cdot y \cdot y} = \dfrac{x^3}{y^3}$

Rule of Zero Exponents: A power raised to the exponent 0 is always equal to 1. For instance, $5^0 = 1$, $100^0 = 1$, and $x^0 = 1$.

This is the case out of mathematical necessity, the mother of invention of nice, little rules like this one. Here's how it happened. As you saw above, when powers are being multiplied, you add the exponents. For example, $x^3 \cdot x^4 = x^7$. So if x^0 were multiplied by x^3, the product would need to be x^3 because 3 would be the sum of the exponents 3 and 0. What can you multiply x^3 by to get x^3? To leave a nonzero number unchanged by multiplication, you need to multiply it by everybody's favorite number: 1, of course. Thus, x^0 must equal 1.

This leads us to the next rule of exponents, which applies to negative exponents.

Rule of Negative Exponents: If $x^3 \cdot x^{-3} = x^0 = 1$, what is x^{-3}?

Well, it must be the reciprocal of x^3, which is $\dfrac{1}{x^3}$, and so it is. When you have a negative exponent, invert the base and raise it to the positive of that exponent.

Exponents are, as you just saw, not so daunting after all. If you ever find yourself confused as to what to do with an exponent in a particular situation, expand it in the way shown above and the rules will in all likelihood become clear.

EXERCISE 3.1

Calculate the following powers and simplify where possible.

1. $(-5)^2$

2. $\left(\left(-\dfrac{1}{3}\right)^2\right)^3$

3. $(x^{-2})^3$

4. $x^3 \cdot x^{-2}$

5. $\dfrac{x^{-4}}{x^2}$

6. $\left(\dfrac{a}{b}\right)^{-3}$

7. $(a^{-2})^{-3}$

8. $\dfrac{x^{-2}}{x^4}$

WAIT, WHAT ABOUT ROOTS?

Finally, there is another form of exponent; the fractional exponent. The fractional exponent is nothing more than an expression of a root. **Roots** are those numbers which, when multiplied together, produce the number in question. Square roots are denoted by a plain radical sign $\sqrt{}$ and they ask: What number, squared (or times itself), is equal to the number under the radical sign? For instance, $\sqrt{16}$ asks what number, squared, is equal to 16? The number under the radical sign is called the **base**; in this case, the base is 16. The square root of 16 is 4, because 4 squared equals 16.

There are all kinds of roots though, not just square, and they are depicted by the **index**, which is a small number next to the radical sign.

$$\text{index} \longrightarrow \sqrt[3]{8} \begin{array}{l} \longleftarrow \text{radical sign} \\ \longleftarrow \text{base} \end{array}$$

For instance, $\sqrt[3]{8}$ represents the cube root of 8, which is 2 (because $2 \cdot 2 \cdot 2 = 8$). The index of this root is 3.

ROOTS AND NEGATIVES

You know from the previous section that while 4^2 is 16, -4^2 is also equal to 16. However, most of the time (but not always), when you're asked for the square root of a number, you're being asked for the positive square root, so $\sqrt{4} = +2$, even though both $+2$ and -2 are the square roots, because if you square either one of them you end up with 4.

When you see a cube root (or another root with an odd-numbered index) with a positive base number, the cube root will be positive. If the base number is negative, the cube root will be negative. For instance, $\sqrt[3]{8} = 2$ because only $+2^3$ is equal to 8, while $\sqrt[3]{-64} = -4$, because only a negative number cubed will result in a negative base.

And what, you may ask, is the square root of a negative number? Well, most squares of negative numbers that you see will be expressed as factors of $\sqrt{-1}$. For instance, $\sqrt{-3}$ is expressed as $\sqrt{3} \cdot \sqrt{-1}$. And what is $\sqrt{-1}$?

$$\sqrt{-1} = i$$

The square root of negative one is not a real number; it's known as an imaginary number, or i. This number, i, figures prominently in higher branches of mathematics, and its appearance means that whatever problem you're working on contains elements that are outside the set of real numbers. Expressions in which i is combined by multiplication or division with real numbers are called complex numbers. If you see them, $(a + bi)$ for instance, be aware that i can be multiplied, divided, and generally treated just like any other number. It just happens to be imaginary. And if you're lucky enough to end up with i^2 after factoring, multiplying, or performing any other operations, remember that i^2 is equal to -1. Imaginary numbers are, of course, a compelling subject, but they're not really relevant at this level of algebra. When you venture further into mathematics, engineering, and science you may see them pop up again.

BUT HEY, WE WERE TALKING ABOUT FRACTIONAL EXPONENTS!

How is all this related to fractional exponents, you ask? Well, a fractional exponent is another way of representing a root; the number in the denominator of the fraction shows the index of the root. For instance, $16^{\frac{1}{2}}$ is the same thing as $\sqrt{16}$; the exponent $\frac{1}{2}$ represents a square root. And $27^{\frac{1}{3}}$ is the same as $\sqrt[3]{27}$; they both represent the cube root of 27.

A fractional exponent is another way of representing a root; the number in the denominator of the fraction shows the index of the root.

What happens if the exponent is a fraction in which the numerator is not 1, for instance $8^{\frac{2}{3}}$? Like any other math challenge, take it step by step in the pieces you know. The denominator of this fraction, 3, shows that a cube root is asked for, and the numerator of this fraction, 2, shows that when the cube root is found, it should be squared. We can write it like this:

$$8^{\frac{2}{3}} = 8^{\frac{1}{3} \times \frac{2}{1}} = \left(\sqrt[3]{8}\right)^2$$

Now, what is the cube root of 8? It's 2. And what is 2 squared? It's 4. Thus, $8^{\frac{2}{3}}$ equals 4.

SQUARING SQUARE ROOTS

Squaring a square root results in the number under the radical sign, as long as that number is greater than or equal to 0. For instance as long as x is greater than or equal to $0, \left(\sqrt{x}\right)^2$ equals x. Or numerically, $\left(\sqrt{16}\right)^2$ equals 16.

SQUARE ROOTS AND ABSOLUTE VALUE

What is the result of a square root of a squared number, for example $\sqrt{a^2}$? The square root of a squared number results in the **absolute value** of the number itself.

Sound confusing? It isn't, really. First, though, you ought to know what absolute value is: The absolute value of a number is the distance on the number line between that number and 0, and that distance is always positive. The symbol for absolute value looks like this: $|a|$, two vertical bars on either side of the number. The absolute value of a is a if $a \geq 0$, and $-a$ if a is a negative number, or $a < 0$; thus the absolute value of -2 (written $|-2|$) is 2; the absolute value of 3, or $|3|$, is 3.

As we said above, the square root of a squared number results in the absolute value of the number itself: $\sqrt{a^2}$ is equal to $|a|$. You can see it numerically: $\sqrt{4^2}$ is equal to 4 because $\sqrt{16}$ is equal to 4. Also, $\sqrt{-3^2} = \sqrt{9} = 3$ which is $|-3|$.

OTHER RULES OF ROOTS

Roots with like bases and indexes can be added or subtracted. For example, $3\sqrt{2} + 5\sqrt{2} = 8\sqrt{2}$.

Think of these literally as three groups of $\sqrt{2}$, combined with five groups of $\sqrt{2}$. How many groups is that total? Eight.

Roots of positive numbers can be multiplied and divided, even if they have different bases. For instance, $\sqrt{4} \times \sqrt{6} = \sqrt{24}$, and $\dfrac{\sqrt{15}}{\sqrt{3}} = \sqrt{5}$.

Example

What is $3\sqrt{2} \times \sqrt{8}$?

All you have to do here is multiply the roots. You get 3 times $\sqrt{2}$ times $\sqrt{8}$, or 3 times $\sqrt{16}$. Of course, you happen to know that $\sqrt{16}$ is 4, so you have 3 times 4, or 12. And there's your answer.

Example

Let's try one more where the roots have coefficients. What is $3\sqrt{5} \times 2\sqrt{2}$?

Multiply the roots and their coefficients. You get $6\sqrt{10}$. There's your answer, no muss, no fuss.

SIMPLIFYING SQUARE ROOTS

Knowing the ways in which roots can be multiplied and divided will help you simplify them. For instance, $\sqrt{50}$ can also be seen as $\sqrt{25 \times 2}$, which, as you saw above, is the same as $\sqrt{25} \times \sqrt{2}$. You can take the square root of the 25 and leave the 2 beneath the radical sign to get $5\sqrt{2}$.

RATIONALIZING THE DENOMINATOR

There will also be cases in which you have a root as the denominator of a fraction. You can get rid of roots and other complicated denominators by **rationalizing** them. We'll show you how to do it; say you have this:

$$\frac{a}{\sqrt{x}}$$

You want to have a rational denominator; who wouldn't? So you multiply the whole fraction by 1 in the form of the radical over the radical, since this is a square root.

$$\frac{a}{\sqrt{x}} \times \frac{\sqrt{x}}{\sqrt{x}} = \frac{a\sqrt{x}}{\sqrt{x}^2} = \frac{a\sqrt{x}}{x}$$

Ta da! This will work with any radical denominator, but remember to pay attention to the index of the root. If it is a cube root you will need to multiply it yet another time. For example, to rationalize $\frac{2}{\sqrt[3]{3}}$ you must multiply $\sqrt[3]{3}$ by itself twice to make it a whole number.

$$\frac{2}{\sqrt[3]{3}} \times \frac{\left(\sqrt[3]{3}\right)^2}{\left(\sqrt[3]{3}\right)^2} \text{ becomes } \frac{2\sqrt[3]{9}}{3}$$

Roots are wonderful. Care to try some?

EXERCISE 3.2

Solve or simplify the following terms and expressions.

1. $\sqrt[3]{125}$

2. $18^{\frac{1}{2}}$

3. $16^{-\frac{4}{3}}$

4. $\dfrac{5^{\frac{3}{2}} \times 5^{-1} \times 5^{-2}}{5^{-2} \times 5^{\frac{4}{5}} \times 5^{\frac{2}{3}} \times 5^{-\frac{7}{15}}}$

5. $\sqrt{x^3}$

6. $\left(x^2 y^3 27\right)^{\frac{1}{3}}$

7. $\left(x^{\frac{1}{2}} y^2\right) \times \left(x^2 y^{\frac{1}{2}}\right)$

8. $\left(\dfrac{a^2 b}{x^{-2} y}\right)^{\frac{1}{2}}$

ANSWERS TO CHAPTER THREE EXERCISES

EXERCISE 3.1 ANSWERS

1. 25

2. $\dfrac{1}{729}$

3. $\dfrac{1}{x^6}$

4. x

   When multiplying powers with the same base, simply add the exponents. In this case they add up to 1, so you get x^1, which is equal to x.

5. $\dfrac{1}{x^6}$

   To divide powers with the same base, simply subtract the exponents. In this case you have –4 minus 2 which is –6, so you get x^{-6}, which you know from question 3 is $\dfrac{1}{x^6}$.

6. $\left(\dfrac{b}{a}\right)^3$

   When a number (or variable) is raised to a negative power, simply invert the number and raise it to the positive power. Here you have $\left(\dfrac{a}{b}\right)^{-3}$. So what you really have is $\dfrac{1}{\left(\dfrac{a}{b}\right)^3}$, which is $\left(\dfrac{b}{a}\right)^3$.

7. a^6

   This may have given you pause. Of course you know when raising an exponent to another exponent you simply multiply the exponents, and in this case that would give you an answer of positive 6. But how could that be, you might have asked yourself. Well, go through it step by step; it's very similar to the previous question. First, a^{-2} is $\dfrac{1}{a^2}$. Then, that raised to another negative, –3, is $\dfrac{1}{\left(a^2\right)^3}$. The way you divide a fraction that looks like that is to multiply the top by the inverse of the denominator. In this case, $1 \times \dfrac{\left(a^2\right)^3}{1} = a^6$.

8. x^{-6} or $\dfrac{1}{x^6}$

EXERCISE 3.2 ANSWERS

1. 5

2. $3\sqrt{2}$

   This takes a bit of factoring. By thinking around for a perfect square factor of 18, you can find that 9 is a factor of 18, so $\sqrt{9}$, along with $\sqrt{2}$, is a factor of $\sqrt{18}$. You can take the square root of the 9 and get $3\sqrt{2}$.

3. $\dfrac{1}{32\sqrt[3]{2}}$ or $\dfrac{\sqrt[3]{4}}{64}$

   Look at the exponent on 16 as having two parts: the fraction $\dfrac{1}{3}$, which means you are looking for a cube root, and –4, which makes the 16 really a fraction, $\dfrac{1}{16}$, which is raised to the 4th power. You can then set it up like so: $\dfrac{1}{\sqrt[3]{16^4}}$. This can be also seen as $\dfrac{1}{\sqrt[3]{16 \times 16 \times 16 \times 16}}$. Behold, there's a cube root in there! There are four 16's; you can take three of them out as a cube root, and multiply the leftover radical by 16: $\dfrac{1}{16\left(\sqrt[3]{16}\right)}$.

   Now, can the leftover 16 be simplified? Well, it can also be written as $3\sqrt{8} \times \sqrt[3]{2}$, and since the cube root of 8 is 2, you get $\dfrac{1}{16 \times 2\sqrt[3]{2}}$, which is also known as $\dfrac{1}{32\sqrt[3]{2}}$. To rationalize the denominator you must multiply it not just once by the same radical, but twice, because it's a cube root. You get $\dfrac{1}{32\sqrt[3]{2}} \times \dfrac{\sqrt[3]{2}}{\sqrt[3]{2}} \times \dfrac{\sqrt[3]{2}}{\sqrt[3]{2}}$, which equals $\dfrac{\sqrt[3]{4}}{32 \times 2}$, which equals $\dfrac{\sqrt[3]{4}}{64}$. Take these slow and step by step and you will prevail.

4. $\dfrac{\sqrt{5}}{5}$

Here you can really use the rules of exponents to your advantage. First you can cancel the 5^{-2}'s, then you can follow the other rules. In the numerator, simply add the exponents since powers of the same base are being multiplied. You find that $\frac{3}{2}$ plus -1 is $\frac{1}{2}$, so the top is $5^{\frac{1}{2}}$, or $\sqrt{5}$. The bottom may look daunting, but again, to multiply powers of the same base simply add the exponents. Here, $\frac{4}{5} + \frac{2}{3} = \frac{22}{15}$, and $\frac{22}{15} + \left(-\frac{7}{15}\right) = \frac{15}{15}$, or 1. Thus, you end up with a much simpler denominator, 5^{-1} or just 5, and a much simpler fraction, $\frac{\sqrt{5}}{5}$.

5. $x\sqrt{x}$

6. $3y\left(\sqrt[3]{x^2}\right)$

   Each number or variable within the parentheses in this question is raised to the $\frac{1}{3}$, meaning that the cube root is taken of each. The cube root of y^3 is y, of 27 is 3, and of x^2 is $\sqrt[3]{x^2}$.

7. $(xy)^{\frac{5}{2}}$

8. $\dfrac{|a|x\sqrt{b}}{\sqrt{y}}$ or $\dfrac{|a|x\sqrt{b}\sqrt{y}}{y}$

   Since all of this is raised to the power of $\frac{1}{2}$, you must take the square root of the whole shebang. The square root of a^2 results in the absolute value of a, or $|a|$. The x of the denominator is being raised to a negative power and so should be flipped to the top; then, since its square root is also taken (and since it's a square), it ends up as its absolute value. Both b and y are simply square roots, but you can rationalize the denominator if you like, by multiplying the whole mess by $\sqrt{y}$.

Logarithms

As you well know by now, $3^2 = 9$.

You also know that if you see $3^2 = a$, then $a = 9$. And if you have $a^2 = 9$, then $a = 3$ (if you knew that a was restricted to being positive). And even if you saw something you don't always see, $3^a = 9$, you would know that $a = 2$.

This last equation introduces you to another way of approaching exponents: **logarithms**. Logarithms express exponential equations in terms of a base and a result that are set equal to the exponent. For example: $\log_3 9 = a$ is the same as $3^a = 9$.

We can look at it with all the numbers filled in.

$$\log_3 9 = 2$$

Three is the **base** of the logarithm in this case, and the whole expression is said to be "the logarithm of 9 to the base three."

The base, 3, raised to the power 2 gives you that term in the middle, 9. You could express this relationship even more elaborately:

$$\log_3 (3^2) = 2$$

This expresses the truth of all logarithms: *The number or term next to the base is always the result of the base raised to the number that the equation is set equal to.*

Logarithms can only be used in cases where the base is greater than 0 and not equal to 1. Negative numbers and zero do not have logarithms.

So a logarithm allows the equation to be expressed as solving for the exponent rather than the value of the power. This, we promise you, will make certain future mathematical operations easier, or we wouldn't make you go through the trouble of learning it. Let's look at that equivalence again:

$$3^2 = 9 \text{ is the same as } \log_3 9 = 2$$

More generally, $x^a = y$ is the same as $\log_x y = a$.
Try it with some other powers.

$$4^a = 16 \text{ is the same as } a = \log_4 16$$
$$4^2 = 16 \text{ is the same as } 2 = \log_4 16$$
$$5^3 = 125 \text{ is the same as } 3 = \log_5 125$$
$$4^{\frac{1}{2}} = 2 \text{ is the same as } \frac{1}{2} = \log_4 2$$

As you can see, you already know the basics of logarithms because you know the basics of exponents. But just to make sure, try converting the next few expressions: If they are in the form of powers, make them into logarithms and solve them and if they are in the form of logarithms, convert them into powers.

EXERCISE 4.1

1. $6^5 = 7{,}776$

2. $3^2 = 9$

3. $\left(\dfrac{1}{2}\right)^3 = \dfrac{1}{8}$

4. $7^0 = 1$

5. $\log_3 81 = 4$

6. $\log_5 5 = 1$

7. $\log_5 1 = 0$

8. $\log_5 0.04 = -2$

THE RULES OF LOGARITHMS

As you can imagine, the rules of logarithms are essentially the same as the rules for powers and exponents. First let's learn the rules for the logarithm of a product.

Since $\log_3 9 = 2$ can also be written as $\log_3 (3^2) = 2$, we can say, more generally, that $\log_3 (3^x) = x$. So if $\log_3 (3^2 \cdot 3^3) = x$, what is x? Since 3 is the base, the exponent that the whole logarithm is set equal to must be the sum of the exponents that the 3 is raised to within the parentheses. This means that the answer must be 5, since $(3^2 \cdot 3^3)$ is a base of 3 being raised to the 5th power. (Remember the rule of multiplying exponents?)

Logarithmically this means:

$$\log_3 (3^x \cdot 3^y) = x + y$$

Since $\log_3 (3^x) = x$, and $\log_3 (3^y) = y$, you know that $x + y = \log_3 (3^x) + \log_3 (3^y)$.

$$\log_3 (3^x \cdot 3^y) = \log_3 (3^x) + \log_3 (3^y)$$

All of the above expressions are equivalent, but the last one most clearly demonstrates the multiplication property of logarithms. The general algebraic form of this property is as follows:

$$\log_a xy = \log_a x + \log_a y$$

For a logarithm of base a where $a > 0$ and $a \neq 1$, the logarithm of the product of two numbers (above we use x and y) is equal to the sum of each of their logarithms.

The next rule regards division. As you well know, when powers of the same base are divided, their exponents are subtracted. What is x if $\log_3 \left(\dfrac{3^6}{3^2} \right) = x$?

We see that x must be $\log_3 (3^4)$, or 4. Thus $\log_3 \left(\dfrac{3^x}{3^y} \right) = x - y$. As you know, $\log_3 3^x = x$, and $\log_3 3^y = y$, thus $\log_3 \left(\dfrac{3^x}{3^y} \right) = x - y = \log_3 (3^x) - \log_3 (3^y)$.

Algebraically then, the expression of the logarithmic property of a quotient is this:

$$\log_a \frac{y}{x} = \log_a y - \log_a x$$

The final rule of logarithms that you need to know is the rule regarding logarithms with exponents in them. Seeing as you're so familiar with logarithms of base 3, we'll use one of those. As you've already seen, $\log_3 (3^2) = 2$. Well, you could also express this as $2\log_3 3 = 2$ (the exponent that 3 needs to be raised to in order to yield 3 is 1). This works with larger exponents; actually it works for all exponents (that's why it's a general property, right?). How about simplifying $\log_3 (27^2)$? It's $2\log_3 27$. Which, by the way, is 6. This follows from the rules of raising exponents, of course! When you raise an exponent to another power you multiply the exponents. Thus, the logarithmic equation that produces the exponent is multiplied by the new exponent.

The algebraic expression of this general property is this:

$$\log_a (x^y) = y \log_a x$$

Example

What is $\log_3 (9^{27})$?

Here we can use the property of logarithms and exponents. That means going from $\log_3 (9^{27})$ to $27\log_3 9$. Now, what is $\log_3 9$? What power is the base 3 raised to that yields 9? It's raised to the second power, of course, so 27(2) is the answer, or 54.

Now work through a few logarithms on your own, referring back to the rules for assistance and clarity.

EXERCISE 4.2

Solve for the unknown in the following.

1. $\log_3 81 = x$

2. $\log_x 36 = 2$

3. $\log_7 343 = x$

4. $\log_4 x = 2.5$

5. $\log_x .01 = -2$

6. $\log_3 \dfrac{27 \cdot 9 \cdot 81}{243} = x$

7. $\log_2 \sqrt{32} = x$

8. $\log_7 1 = x$

ANSWERS TO CHAPTER FOUR EXERCISES

ANSWERS TO EXERCISE 4.1

1. $\log_6 7{,}776 = 5$

2. $\log_3 9 = 2$

3. $\log_{\frac{1}{2}} \frac{1}{8} = 3$

4. $\log_7 1 = 0$

5. $3^4 = 81$

6. $5^1 = 5$

7. $5^0 = 1$

8. $5^{-2} = 0.04$

ANSWERS TO EXERCISE 4.2

1. $x = 4$

2. $x = 6$

3. $x = 3$

4. $x = 32$
   This might have taken a few steps; it says that the exponent 4 is raised to is 2.5, which means there's a fractional exponent, a root. You can convert it into a fraction of $\frac{5}{2}$, or raise 4 to the fifth power and then take the square root.

5. $x = 10$

6. $x = 4$
   You can look at the rules of logs for this; they indicate that the logarithim of a quotient is found by subtracting the logarithms, as they can be here. The way to do this easily is to convert the fraction into powers of 3.

7. $x = 2.5$
   You must recognize that $\sqrt{32}$ can be expressed as a power of 2. Change the 32 into a power of 2, so it's 2^5. Then the square root is expressed as a fractional exponent.

8. $x = 0$

CHAPTER 5

Polynomials

Okay, now is the time for us to admit having held back information. The expressions you've been working with have certain special names: **monomials, binomials, trinomials,** and **polynomials.** Don't they sound impressive? Now you can casually drop these names in conversation. But what is a monomial, you ask? A monomial expression is an expression consisting of only one term. *Mono* is a prefix meaning one, like *monologue* or *monocle.* Some examples of monomials are $3x^2$, $17x$, and $a^2 b^2 c$.

So what is a binomial, then? An expression having two terms, *bi* as in *bi*focals, *bi*sexual, or *bi*cycle. For instance, $3x + 2$ is a binomial, so are $a^2b - bc$, and $3xy - xy^2$. Trinomials are expressions of three terms, such as $3x^2 - 2x + 5$.

Polynomials, by strict definition, are expressions that contain more than one term; algebraic expressions put together from variables and numbers by means of addition, subtraction, and multiplication. Polynomials include binomials, trinomials, and other multiterm expressions, but generally people use the term *polynomial* to refer to any old algebraic expression, even a monomial. Go figure.

Polynomials comprise most of what you work with in algebra, and they come in specific types called degrees. When the **degree** of a polynomial or a monomial is indicated, it refers to the exponent involved. A polynomial without a visible exponent is an expression of degree one, because lack of a visible exponent means that any term or variable can be said to be raised to the first power. The number of the exponent gives the degree. For instance, the monomial $4x^2y$ is a monomial of degree 2, because the exponent of the x is 2. If there is more than one exponent involved in an expression, as in the polynomial $3x^2y - x + y^3$, then the degree of the expression is the highest degree present, which in this case is the 3 from the term y^3.

In a monomial—and only in a monomial—of more than one variable the naming method is somewhat different. The degree of a monomial of this type is the sum of the exponents. For instance, $6x^2y^3$ is a monomial of two different variables with two different exponents. In this case, the degree is 5.

TYPES OF POLYNOMIALS

Degrees can also give names to particular classes of polynomials. **Linear polynomials** are polynomials of degree 1, mostly in the form of $ax + b$, where a is a nonzero number, for instance $5x + 7$, or $3x - 1$.

Quadratic polynomials are those of degree 2, usually in the form $ax^2 + bx + c$, where a is a nonzero number, for instance $x^2 + 2x + 4$, or $2x^2 + 3x$ (in which $c = 0$).

ADDING POLYNOMIALS

You already know that you can combine like terms, that you can use the distributive property to multiply terms, and that you can perform all sorts of wonderful feats with powers (like multiply them by adding their exponents). All of this knowledge will be useful when you're dealing with polynomials.

To add polynomials, simply combine like terms of the same degree. To add the polynomials $4x^2 - 3x + 7$ and $3x^3 - 5x^2 + 2x - 1$, stack the polynomials so the like terms are aligned, and combine them as the various signs instruct.

$$
\begin{array}{r}
3x^3 - 5x^2 + 2x - 1 \\
+\quad\ \ 4x^2 - 3x + 7 \\
\hline
3x^3 - x^2 - x + 6
\end{array}
$$

So the sum of the two polynomials is $3x^3 - x^2 - x + 6$. The same approach works for subtraction; stack them up and subtract their like terms.

OPERATIONS FOR BINOMIALS

To add binomials, stack them as you just saw the polynomials above stacked, and combine like terms. So how does one multiply binomials? By using the good old distributive property, which can be simplified for binomials into one handy little acronym: **FOIL**. FOIL stands for First Outside Inside Last, which is the order in which you multiply the terms within binomials to make sure you don't miss one. For instance, $(x + 5)$ times $(2x - 2)$. Multiply the terms in the order **FOIL**.

First: $(x + 5)(2x - 2) = 2x^2$

Outside: $(x + 5)(2x - 2) = 2x^2 - 2x$

Inside: $(x + 5)(2x - 2) = 2x^2 - 2x + 10x$

Last: $(x + 5)(2x - 2) = 2x^2 - 2x + 10x - 10$

Combine the like terms, and you have your product.

$$2x^2 - 2x + 10x - 10 \text{ becomes } 2x^2 + 8x - 10$$

MULTIPLYING POLYNOMIALS

Multiplying more extended polynomials is essentially the same as multiplying binomials, it just takes longer. You go from the first term on through all the terms, however many there may be.

Example

Multiply the following two polynomials.

$$\left(3x^2 + 2x - 4\right)\left(5x^3 - 3x^2 + 4x + 2\right)$$

Here we go. Start with the first polynomial, and multiply its first term by each term in the second polynomial, then do the same for the next term, and so on.

$$\left[15x^5 - 9x^4 + 12x^3 + 6x^2\right] + \left[10x^4 - 6x^3 + 8x^2 + 4x\right] + \left[-20x^3 + 12x^2 - 16x - 8\right]$$

Whew. Now all you have to do is combine the like terms. You can do this easily by stacking up the results of your multiplication as you go along instead of stringing them out.

$$
\begin{aligned}
15x^5 - 9x^4 + 12x^3 +\ & 6x^2 \\
10x^4 - 6x^3 +\ & 8x^2 + 4x \\
+\qquad\qquad\quad -20x^3 +\ & 12x^2 - 16x - 8 \\
\hline
15x^5 +\ x^4 - 14x^3 + 26x^2 -\ & 12x - 8
\end{aligned}
$$

Pretty cool. Now, what degree is the final expression? Why, it's an expression of degree 5 of course; 5 is the highest level exponent around, and not coincidentally, the sum of the highest degree of each of the two original expressions.

EXERCISE 5.1

Add, subtract, or multiply the following polynomials as instructed.

1. $(x + 5)(x - 3)$

2. $(x - 1)(3x^3 - 2x^2 + 5x - 1)$

3. $(6x^2 + 3x + 2) - (4x^3 + 5x^2 - 7x + 1)$

4. $(x^3 + 1)(x^2 - 1)$

5. $(5x^4 - 4x^3 - 3x^2 - 2x - 1)(5x^4 + 4x^3 + 3x^2 + 2x + 1)$

6. $(x + 1)(x^3 - x^2 - x - 1)$

7. $(7x^4 + 6x^3 + 5x^2 + 3x + 2) + (-7x^4 - 6x^3 + 5x^2 + 3x + 2)$

8. $(x - 1)(x^4 - x^3 - x^2 - x - 1)$

FACTORING

You know how to multiply polynomials, and it seems reasonable to assume that factoring them can't be much more difficult. You should understand that while some polynomials appear daunting, they are often easy to manipulate. You already factored a number of polynomials in the previous sections. Remember your exercise with the distributive law on page 11? There, you removed the common factor of a polynomial whether it was a numerical coefficient or a variable that appeared in all the terms. This is the way to start when factoring any polynomial. For instance, the following polynomial has a factor common to each term.

$$3x^2 + 12x + 9$$

As you may have already recognized, 3 is the common factor of each term, and you can factor it out.

$$3\left(x^2 + 4x + 3\right)$$

The way to factor polynomials further than this is to determine what expressions were multiplied to yield the degrees and terms in question. For instance, when you have a trinomial like the one inside the parentheses above, in which the first term is a perfect square, you can sometimes factor it by looking at its terms. We'll start with the inner trinomial presented above, whose first term is a square with coefficient one.

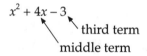

$$x^2 + 4x - 3$$
third term
middle term

Since the first term, x^2, is a square, it is the product of two first degree polynomials. The first step in factoring a trinomial whose first term is a square is to set up its factors as two first degree binomials.

$$x^2 + 4x + 3$$
$$(x \quad)(x \quad)$$

The second step involves looking at the second and third terms of the trinomial; you need to list the factors of the third term in order to determine which pair of those factors will go in your parentheses. Are they −3 and −1 or 3 and 1? The way to decide this is to determine which factors add up to give the middle coefficient. Since the factors must give the sum positive 4—the middle of the expression is positive $4x$—the signs are plus signs, because the factors that add to give 4 are positive 3 and positive 1.

$$(x + 3)(x + 1)$$

To test your factoring, you should always multiply out and make sure it works.

$$(x+3)(x+1) = x^2 + x + 3x + 3 = x^2 + 4x + 3$$

The way to factor trinomials in which the first term is a square:

Step One: Set up parentheses in which the first terms multiply to form the first, squared term.

Step Two: Look at the third term and list its factors.

Step Three: Choose the correct pair by determining which factors, when added, give the middle term.

Try factoring another trinomial, using the steps outlined above.

$$x^2 - x - 6$$

Step One: Set up the parentheses that result in the first term.

$$(x \quad)(x \quad)$$

Step Two: Look at the third term of the trinomial and list its factors. The factors of -6 are $(-1, 6)$, $(1, -6)$, $(2, -3)$, or $(-2, 3)$. Which ones add up to form the middle coefficient, -1?

Step Three: Decide on the factors and put them in the parentheses. To combine to a middle coefficient of -1, the factors must $(2, -3)$.

$$(x - 3)(x + 2)$$

Now, multiply through to make sure you're okay.

$(x - 3)(x + 2)$ becomes $x^2 + 2x - 3x - 6$ becomes $x^2 - x - 6$, so the factorization is correct.

SQUARED BINOMIALS

Certain trinomials such as $x^2 + 6x + 9$ are particularly wonderful to factor. Why? Both their first and last terms are perfect squares, and since you're expert at factoring at this point, you have probably already noted that the middle term is the sum of the square root of the third term. This means that this trinomial is the product of a squared binomial. Your binomials are going to look like this:

$$(x + 3)(x + 3)$$

Actually, your factoring could even look like this: $(x + 3)^2$

Of course, the first and third terms could be perfect squares and the middle term could be subtracted. What would you do then?

$$x^2 - 6x + 9$$

It seems pretty clear, doesn't it? To get the positive 9 as well as the subtracted $6x$, there must have been a negative multiplied by a negative. It's still a squared binomial, it's just that it's a squared *subtracted* binomial. Try it and see.

$(x - 3)(x - 3)$ becomes $x^2 - 3x - 3x + 9$ becomes $x^2 - 6x + 9$.

The factorization of $x^2 - 6x + 9$ is $(x - 3)^2$

ALMOST SQUARED

Every now and again you'll run into a crazy little polynomial that looks like this:

$$x^2 - 36$$

What you have here is an eminently factorable polynomial, because its terms are both perfect squares, and—here's the key—the second term is a negative. That means that it is the result of a negative and a positive factor. So, the binomial factors look like so:

$$(x + 6)(x - 6)$$

Multiply it out and see what happens.

$(x + 6)(x - 6)$ becomes $x^2 + 6x - 6x - 36$ which becomes $x^2 - 36$.

These expressions are called the difference of perfect squares.

FUNKY TRINOMIALS

Trinomials that are the product of a squared binomial can appear even when the coefficient of the first squared term isn't 1, but is another squared term.

$$9x^2 + 30x + 25$$

Here you can see right off that the first and third terms are perfect squares, and thus you can set up your parentheses calmly, even though you are internally shaken by the appearance of that 9 by your usually humble x^2. Set the binomials up just as you might imagine, with the first terms in the parentheses the root factors of $9x^2$, and the second terms the root factors of 25.

$$(3x + 5)(3x + 5)$$

Multiply it out and you'll see that you've got it. Notice that the middle term was twice the product of the square root of the first term and the square root of the second term. In other words, $(3x)(5) = 15x$, and $(15x)(2) = 30x$, your middle term. This information will be useful in the future.

OTHER TRINOMIALS

Yes, we admit it, there are other trinomials whose first terms have more daunting coefficients. Trinomials that are not products of squared binomials and which begin with a squared term whose coefficient is not equal to 1 are approached as regular trinomials, with a slight difference—a lot more trial and error.

$$4x^2 + 14x + 12$$

The method is a bit of a pain in the neck. It's easy enough to start, by setting up binomial pairs, only this time the first terms are not just x but whatever terms will provide the first term of the trinomial, either the first term's square roots, or its other factors. Here we'll try the square root first for simplicity's sake.

$$(2x \quad)(2x \quad)$$

Step two, as usual, asks you look at the third term and its factor. The second term's coefficient in this case is not as simple as the sum of those factors, however, due to the added twist of the first term's coefficient. Essentially you must experiment with pairs of factors to find an answer. The factors of 12 are (1,12), (2, 6) and (3, 4); since the middle term is not subtracted (it is not a negative number), we will assume that the factors are positive. Try the first pair.

$$(2x + 12)(2x + 1)$$

Now, multiply through to check it.

$$(2x + 12)(2x + 1)$$
$$4x^2 + 2x + 24x + 12$$
$$4x^2 + 26x + 12$$

Not quite, but don't worry, it provides us with some clues. Since you're adding the product of the factors and the $2x$'s, and the $24x$ you got is far too big, you probably want to avoid any large factors such as 6, and try (3, 4) instead.

$(2x + 4)(2x + 3)$ becomes $4x^2 + 6x + 8x + 12$, which becomes $4x^2 + 14x + 12$.

You have the correct factors. Of course, if you had tried 2 and 6, it wouldn't have worked and you would have found the right answer eventually; it just would have taken you a bit longer, all the while providing you with some extra experience in multiplying algebraic terms. Hey, trial-and-error factoring can be seen as a win-win situation if you look at it the right way!

THE BASIC FORMS OF FACTORING

Now that you've worked through a number of factoring problems on your own, take a look at the general ways in which they can be expressed algebraically. Most of these you saw above, but it's nice to see them expressed in general terms. Algebra can be a pretty useful thing, wouldn't you say?

$(x + y)(x + y)$ becomes $x^2 + 2xy + y^2$

$(x + y)(x - y)$ becomes $x^2 - y^2$

$(x - y)(x - y)$ becomes $x^2 - 2xy + y^2$

$(x + y)(x + z)$ becomes $x^2 + (y + z)x + yz$

$(ax + y)(bx + z)$ becomes $abx^2 + (az + by)x + yz$

These general truths can be extremely useful to you, either as ways to factor expressions or as ways to expand them. Become very familiar with them—dare we say it?—memorize them. But before you facilitate your memorization by doing exercise two, there's something you might want to know about rationalizing denominators.

RATIONALIZING AND FACTORING: MORE THAN COINCIDENCE?

You already know how to rationalize the denominator of a fraction, that is, you know how to make sure the denominator of a fraction doesn't have a radical sign. If this doesn't seem quite familiar, look back to page 37 to refresh your memory. But what if your fraction doesn't have just a radical sign, but a radical sign within an expression? Factoring can help when you need to rationalize this type of denominator.

$$\frac{3}{3-\sqrt{2}}$$

How does one eliminate this radical sign? Think about your factoring and expansion formulas; you want the second term of that expression to lose its radical, but you can't multiply it all just by the radical because then the first term will adhere to it. You could square the bottom, but that would give you $9 - 6 + \sqrt{2}$, meaning you still have your old radical sign in the way. Are you getting any ideas? The trick is to remember your factoring formulas: $(x - y)(x + y)$.

If you multiply the whole fraction by 1 in the form of $\dfrac{3+\sqrt{2}}{3+\sqrt{2}}$ a wonderful thing happens to your denominator.

$$\frac{3}{3-\sqrt{2}} \times \frac{3+\sqrt{2}}{3+\sqrt{2}} \text{ becomes } \frac{9+3\sqrt{2}}{9-2} \text{ becomes } \frac{9+3\sqrt{2}}{7}$$

Voila. A rational denominator created by using your combined skills in factoring and roots. Very nice.

EXERCISE 5.2

Factor the following expressions.

1. $x^2 + 2x - 24$
2. $x^2 - 3x + 2$
3. $x^2 + 7x + 12$
4. $x^2 + 10x + 25$
5. $x^2 - 64$
6. $x^2 - 14x + 49$
7. $16x^2 + 24x + 9$
8. $9x^2 - 3x - 20$

WHAT TO DO ONCE YOU'VE FACTORED

Why does one factor? Well, there are any number of reasons. Perhaps you wanted to simplify an expression further; perhaps someone walking down the street began pestering you about how to multiply binomials; perhaps you were asked to factor on an algebra test. In addition to these possibilities, there is yet another reason for factoring: equations. You are familiar with linear equations such as $10 = 2x + 4$. To solve these equations you merely isolate the variable. In this case, $x = 3$. But what if you were given an equation such as $x^2 - 4x - 12 = 0$; a quadratic equation?

SOLVING QUADRATIC EQUATIONS BY FACTORING

When you are given a quadratic equation—that means, generally, an equation of the second degree with only one variable—the first step towards solving it is to put it in the form $ax^2 + bx + c = 0$ in which a is a nonzero number. Sometimes it is already in that wonderful form, as is the equation $x^2 - 4x - 12 = 0$. (The reason that a trinomial in which there are subtraction signs can still be viewed as being in the form $ax^2 + bx + c = 0$ is that the terms are viewed as $a = 1$, $b = -4$ and $c = -12$, so the subtraction signs fade away.) You may be given equations that look slightly different, such as $2x^2 + 3x = -2x + 7$. In this case, just collect the terms on one side and combine like terms by performing the opposite operations, just as you might if you were trying to isolate a variable.

$$2x^2 + 3x = -2x + 7 \text{ becomes}$$
$$2x^2 + 3x + 2x - 7 = 0 \text{ becomes } 2x^2 + 5x - 7 = 0$$

An equation may have parentheses before you go at it, such as $x(x + 2) - 3 = 0$. If it does, multiply it out until it's in your basic, old $ax^2 + bx + c = 0$ form.

$$x(x + 2) - 3 = 0 \text{ becomes } x^2 + 2x - 3 = 0$$

An equation might have radical signs, such as $\sqrt{4x^2 + 2x} = 3$. If you are confronted with something like this, simply do away with the radical sign by squaring both sides. (See? It's still performing the opposite operation to both sides of the equation.)

$$\left(\sqrt{4x^2 + 2x}\right)^2 = (3)^2 \text{ becomes } 4x^2 + 2x = 9 \text{ becomes } 4x^2 + 2x - 9 = 0$$

And what if you come across a fraction in your precious equation? Think about it for a moment. You know what to do: Again, perform the opposite operation to both sides of the equation.

$$x^2 + x + \frac{1}{4} = 0 \text{ becomes } 4x^2 + 4x + 1 = 0$$

Notice, the 0 on the right side of the equation isn't changed by multiplying it by 4, but be aware that you have still performed the same operation to both sides of the equation.

Once you have your equation in the precious $ax^2 + bx + c = 0$ form, try to factor it. This is the easiest way to solve an equation. If we go back to our first equation, $x^2 - 4x - 12 = 0$, we discover that it can be easily factored. The factors of -12 can be $(1,-12)$, $(-1,12)$, $(2,-6)$, $(-2,6)$, $(3,-4)$ or $(-3,4)$. Which of these pairs gives a sum of -4 for the middle term? Why, $(2,-6)$ of course. You've got this baby factored.

$$(x + 2)(x - 6) = 0$$

The solutions to a quadratic equation like this are called **roots;** they are different from roots as in square roots. You will almost always be able to tell which kind of root is being referred to in a question by the context of the question itself. In this case, what two numbers could x be so that the equation will equal 0? Any number that will make one of these binomial factors equal to 0. Once a factor is 0, the whole equation multiplies out to 0.

What is x such that $(x + 2) = 0$?
What is x such that $(x - 6) = 0$

As you can see, x must be either -2 or 6.
So the roots of the quadratic equation $x^2 - 4x - 12 = 0$ are -2 and 6.

ISN'T THERE ANOTHER WAY TO SOLVE A QUADRATIC EQUATION?

What about equations you can't factor? If you've been thinking to yourself, "I know there's something else, some other way..." you're right. There are other ways to find the solutions for quadratic equations: One such option is called the **quadratic formula**. The quadratic formula states that for that favorite equation of ours, $ax^2 + bx + c = 0$, where a is a nonzero number:

$$x = \frac{-b \pm \sqrt{b^2 - 4ac}}{2a}$$

We can find the roots of the equation we started with here, $x^2 - 4x - 12 = 0$, by the quadratic formula as well as by factoring. In our equation, $a = 1$, $b = -4$, and $c = -12$. We can then put these values into the quadratic equation.

$$\frac{-(-4) \pm \sqrt{(-4)^2 - 4(1)(-12)}}{2(1)}$$

$$\frac{4 \pm \sqrt{16 - (-48)}}{2}$$

$$\frac{4 \pm \sqrt{64}}{2}$$

The two roots of the equation are accounted for by the ± sign. First use the plus part.

$$\frac{4 + 8}{2} \text{ becomes } \frac{12}{2} \text{ becomes } 6$$

With the minus sign, you find the other root of the equation.

$$\frac{4 - 8}{2} \text{ becomes } \frac{-4}{2} \text{ becomes } -2$$

So the roots of the quadratic equation $x^2 - 4x - 12 = 0$ are 6 and –2. Sure, you knew the roots already from factoring, but you can see where the quadratic equation would come in mighty handy if you were unable to factor an equation.

IT WAS JUST MY IMAGINATION, RUNNING AWAY WITH ME...

How about using the quadratic formula to find the roots of the equation $x^2 - 2x + 4 = 0$? In this equation, $a = 1$, $b = -2$, and $c = 4$. Putting these values into the quadratic equation yields

$$\frac{-(-2) \pm \sqrt{(-2)^2 - 4(1)(4)}}{2} \text{ which becomes}$$

$$\frac{2 \pm \sqrt{4 - 16}}{2} \text{ which becomes } \frac{2 \pm \sqrt{-12}}{2}$$

You have a negative square root, now what are you going to do? Well, you are going to simplify it as much as possible, and after that simplification you will note that the answer contains imaginary numbers.

$$\frac{2 \pm \sqrt{4(-3)}}{2}$$

$$\frac{2 \pm 2\sqrt{-3}}{2}$$

The solution is $1 \pm \sqrt{3}\sqrt{-1}$, which can also be written $1 \pm i\sqrt{3}$.

ANOTHER WAY OF SOLVING A QUADRATIC EQUATION: COMPLETING THE SQUARE

You are familiar with trinomials that are perfect squares, meaning that they are the products of squared binomials. (If you aren't, go back to page 54 and become familiar.) You've even factored a few squared binomials in your time, if we remember correctly.

Let's look at a few perfect square trinomials:

$$x^2 + 6x + 9$$
$$x^2 + 4x + 4$$
$$x^2 + 10x + 25$$

Now what groovy thing do all these have in common? Well, yes, for all of them the first term is x^2. And the other commonality, which is true for all perfect trinomial squares, is that the last term is found by squaring one half of the coefficient of x. For example, in the first one, the coefficient of x is 6, half this coefficient is 3, which, when squared, is 9. This relationship between the second and third term holds for all perfect trinomial squares, and makes a lot of sense if you look closely at what happens when you square a binomial.

$(x + 3)(x + 3)$ becomes $x^2 + 3x + 3x + 9$ becomes $x^2 + 6x + 9$

Why is this relationship important? It allows you to perform a funky operation called **completing the square**, which provides you with yet another way of solving trinomials. We'll show you how it works with the equation $x^2 + 10x - 11 = 0$. To complete the square in this situation, reorder the equation so that the first two terms are on one side and the third term is on the other side of the equation.

$x^2 + 10x - 11 = 0$ becomes $x^2 + 10x = 11$

The left side of the equation can now be seen as the first two terms of a perfect square. What is needed to complete this square? Well, as you know, the last term is found by squaring one half of the coefficient of x. Here, half the coefficient of x is 5, and 5 squared is 25. So add the last term, but as you would do with any equation manipulation, add it to both sides of the equation.

$$x^2 + 10x + 25 = 11 + 25$$

Simplify the equation so that the square on the left is clearly presented.

$$(x + 5)^2 = 36$$

Take the square root—of both sides of course—and recognize that the square root of the number has to be given as a plus *and* minus in order to provide the two roots of the equation.

$$x + 5 = \pm 6$$

Now you can solve for either eventuality.

$$x + 5 = 6 \text{ means } x = 1$$
$$x + 5 = -6 \text{ means } x = -11$$

And that's how you complete the square. This works with all sorts of equations, even ones with fractions in them, as you can try with this next problem.

$$x^2 + 7x = 8$$

It's already in a form you can use, and yes, yes, we know you could factor it, but humor us by completing the square instead, as a way of getting some good practice. The left side can be viewed as the perfect square to be completed, which means that the third term must be half of the coefficient of x, squared, or $\dfrac{7}{2}$ squared.

$$x^2 + 7x + \left(\frac{7}{2}\right)^2 = 8 + \left(\frac{7}{2}\right)^2 \text{ becomes } x + 7x + \frac{49}{4} = 8 + \frac{49}{4}$$

Once the left side is in its lovely perfect trinomial square form, you can factor it and add together the right side.

$$\left(x + \frac{7}{2}\right)^2 = \frac{81}{4}$$

Next, take the square root so you can find the roots of this equation.

$$\sqrt{\left(x + \frac{7}{2}\right)^2} = \sqrt{\frac{81}{4}} \text{ becomes } x + \frac{7}{2} = \pm\frac{9}{2}$$

Using both the + and the −, solve for x.

$$x + \frac{7}{2} = \frac{9}{2} \text{ becomes } x = 1$$

$$x + \frac{7}{2} = -\frac{9}{2} \text{ becomes } x = -8$$

The roots of this equation are 1 and −8.

You are now extremely knowledgeable about completing squares. What's more, completing the square is useful not only in solving any number of quadratic equations that come to mind, but also for figuring out how the heck they found that quadratic formula.

HOW THE HECK THE QUADRATIC EQUATION WORKS

First look at a quadratic equation in the form of $ax^2 + bx + c = 0$. To put it into a form in which we can complete the square as we've been doing, we have to make the first term into x^2, so we divide the entire equation by a.

$$\frac{ax^2 + bx + c}{a} = \frac{0}{a} \text{ becomes } x^2 + \frac{b}{a}x + \frac{c}{a} = 0$$

Now we can put it further into the completing the square form by putting x^2 and the coefficient of x on one side, and the rest of the equation on the other.

$$x^2 + \frac{b}{a}x = -\frac{c}{a}$$

We've got the equation just where we want it and now all we have to do is complete the square by adding the square of half of the coefficient of x, which represents the third term.

$$x^2 + \frac{b}{a}x + \left(\frac{b}{2a}\right)^2 = -\frac{c}{a} + \left(\frac{b}{2a}\right)^2$$

We can factor the now-perfect square on the left side, and rearrange the right side.

$$\left(x + \frac{b}{2a}\right)^2 = -\frac{b^2}{4a^2} - \frac{c}{a}$$

To make the right side easier to work with, we find a common denominator and subtract the fractions.

$$\left(x + \frac{b}{2a}\right)^2 = -\frac{b^2 - 4ac}{4a^2}$$

Our next step is to take the square root of both sides, after which we will be able to solve for x to find the roots of the equation.

$$x + \frac{b}{2a} = \pm\frac{\sqrt{b^2 - 4ac}}{2a}$$

Now we solve for x in both cases; the plus and the minus, remember? We can do that by isolating x on the left side of the equation.

$$x = \frac{-b \pm \sqrt{b^2 - 4ac}}{2a}$$

Presto, the quadratic formula.

EXERCISE 5.3

Find the roots of the following equations by factoring, the quadratic formula, or completing the square; whatever your heart desires.

1. $x^2 - 5x + 6 = 0$
2. $x^2 + 4x - 8 = 0$
3. $x(x - 5) = 14$
4. $3x^2 - 2x - 4 = 0$
5. $x^2 - x - 1 = 0$
6. $5x^2 + 7x = 6$
7. $5x^2 = -3x + 14$
8. $x^2 = -4x + 9$

DIVISION OF POLYNOMIALS

Every now and again you will be asked to divide polynomials. This operation is more irritating than it is difficult. Dividing, in fact, generally involves factoring the polynomial. For instance, a question may ask you to divide $x^2 - 5x + 4$ by $x - 1$; you would set up this problem as regular long division.

$$x - 1 \overline{)x^2 - 5x + 4}$$

To proceed through the long division, recognize that the **divisor,** in this case $x - 1$, is going to be divided as one number. Both the expressions serve as entire numbers here; there are no decimal places as in regular long division, you must simply try to find terms that yield the expression under the division sign.

Begin by finding the term that yields the first term of the expression under the sign. What will yield x^2 when multiplied by $x - 1$? The first term must be x.

$$
\begin{array}{r}
x \\
x - 1 \overline{)x^2 - 5x + 4} \\
\underline{x^2 - x}
\end{array}
$$

Go forward as you would in any other long division, and remember to be very careful as to the sign of what is being multiplied, and how it will subtract on the bottom. In this case, if you subtract $-x$ from $-5x$, what will you get? Think about it carefully.

$$
\begin{array}{r}
x \\
x - 1 \overline{)x^2 - 5x + 4} \\
\underline{-\left(x^2 - x\right)} \\
-4x + 4
\end{array}
$$

Then, find the next term that you can multiply the divisor by to yield the final term.

$$
\begin{array}{r}
x - 4 \\
x - 1 \overline{)x^2 - 5x + 4} \\
\underline{-\left(x^2 - x\right)} \\
-4x + 4 \\
\underline{-(-4x + 4)} \\
0
\end{array}
$$

Ta da! The answer to the question, "What is $x^2 - 5x + 4$ divided by $x - 1$?" is $x - 4$. You can check your answer easily by multiplying $x - 1$ by $x - 4$ and getting $x^2 - 5x + 4$. Of course, that is essentially what you would have found if you had factored. But the process of dividing a lovely, factorable polynomial such as this lends you the strength and experience necessary to divide a not-so-evenly factorable polynomial that will leave a remainder, such as this: Divide $6x^2 - 7x + 18$ by $2x - 3$.

First step: Set it up as a long division and put whatever it is you need to form the first term on top.

$$
\begin{array}{r}
3x \\
2x-3\overline{)6x^2 -7x+18} \\
-\left(6x^2 -9x\right) \\
\hline
+2x
\end{array}
$$

Drop down the next term, and put the number on top that will give those terms.

$$
\begin{array}{r}
3x \; + \; 1 \\
2x-3\overline{)6x^2 -7x+18} \\
-\left(6x^2 -9x\right) \\
\hline
2x \; + \; 18 \\
-\left(2x \; - \; 3\right) \\
\hline
+21
\end{array}
$$

You're left with a remainder of 21. Here's what you do when you get a remainder: Place the remainder over the divisor and add it to your quotient.

So, $6x^2 - 7x + 18$ divided by $2x - 3$ is $3x + 1 + \dfrac{21}{2x-3}$.

How do you check something like this? It's easy enough. Simply multiply the quotient without the remainder by the divisor, then add the remainder. Like so:

Does $6x^2 - 7x + 18$ divided by $2x - 3$ result in $3x + 1 + \dfrac{21}{2x-3}$?

$(2x - 3)(3x + 1) = 6x^2 + 2x - 9x - 3$ becomes $6x^2 - 7x - 3$

Then add the remainder, 21.

$6x^2 - 7x - 3 + 21$ becomes $6x^2 - 7x + 18$

Pretty nifty, isn't it?

Of course any polynomial can be divided, not just a trinomial. You operate the same way, dividing until you've moved through the whole polynomial.

Example

What is $8x^2 - 4x + 9$ divided by $2x + 3$?
What's your first step?

$$2x + 3 \overline{)8x^2 - 4x + 9}$$

Set it up, and find the factor of the first term.

$$
\begin{array}{r}
4x \\
2x + 3 \overline{)8x^2 - 4x + 9} \\
-\left(8x^2 + 12x\right) \\
\hline
-16x
\end{array}
$$

Find the next term, and see if there is a remainder.

$$
\begin{array}{r}
4x - 8 \\
2x + 3 \overline{)8x^2 - 4x + 9} \\
-\left(8x^2 + 12x\right) \\
\hline
-16x + 9 \\
-\left(-16x - 24\right) \\
\hline
+33
\end{array}
$$

Put the remainder over the divisor, add it on to your quotient, and you've got the answer: $4x - 8 + \dfrac{33}{2x+3}$. Check your answer by multiplying.

$(2x + 3)(4x - 8) = 8x^2 - 16x + 12x - 24$ becomes $8x^2 - 4x - 24$; add the 33 and you have $8x^2 - 4x + 9$.

Can you see why you just add the numerator of the remainder? You're multiplying it by $2x + 3$, aren't you? Think about it.

DIVIDING POLYNOMIALS THAT HAVE "MISSING" TERMS

Sometimes your **dividend** won't have any first degree terms in it; it might be missing numerical terms, or be strange in some other way. For instance, you might be asked to divide $x^2 + 12$ by $x - 1$.

$$x - 1 \overline{)x^2 + 12}$$

The procedure to follow here is to spread apart the terms in the dividend, in this case $x + 12$, so the division can go on through the "missing" terms.

$$
\begin{array}{r}
x \\
x-1{\overline{\smash{\big)}\,x^2 \phantom{{}+{}} + 12}} \\
-\left(x^2 - x\right) \\
\hline
-x + 12
\end{array}
$$

Then, follow through as you normally would.

$$
\begin{array}{r}
x + 1 \\
x-1{\overline{\smash{\big)}\,x^2 \phantom{{}+{}} + 12}} \\
-\left(x^2 - x\right) \\
\hline
x + 12 \\
-\left(x - 1\right) \\
\hline
13
\end{array}
$$

You have a remainder of 13, so the answer is $x + 1 + \dfrac{13}{x-1}$. Multiply it out to check your work.

$(x - 1)(x + 1) = x^2 + x - x - 1$ becomes $x^2 - 1$, add the 13 and you have $x^2 + 12$.

Try dividing some polynomials on your own.

EXERCISE 5.4

1. $x^2 - 3x + 2$ divided by $x - 2$

2. $3x^2 + 6x - 9$ divided by $x - 3$

3. $4x^2 - 8x + 4$ divided by $2x - 2$

4. $5x^2 - 3x + 5$ divided by $x + 2$

5. $3x^3 - x^2 + 2x - 1$ divided by $x - 1$

6. $x^3 + 36x - 6$ divided by $x - 6$

7. $x^2 - 64$ divided by $x + 8$

8. $x^2 - 3xy + 2y^2$ divided by $x + y$

ANSWERS TO CHAPTER FIVE EXERCISES

ANSWERS TO EXERCISE 5.1

1. $x^2 + 2x - 15$
   Our friend FOIL.

2. $3x^4 - 5x^3 + 7x^2 - 6x + 1$
   First multiply the whole second expression by the first term x, then multiply the whole second expression by the second term -1, then combine all like terms, keeping a sharp eye out for the changes in sign wrought by multiplying by a negative.

3. $-4x^3 + x^2 + 10x + 1$
   The easiest way to approach this is to stack the polynomials so the like terms are directly over one another, like so:

   $$6x^2 + 3x + 2$$
   $$-4x^3 + 5x^2 - 7x + 1$$

   This way you can subtract like terms easily, seeing which signs the subtraction affects and which it doesn't.

4. $x^5 - x^3 + x^2 - 1$
   Simply multiply each term, using the impeccable skills you've accumulated with regard to exponents, in the FOIL order.

5. $25x^8 - 16x^6 - 24x^5 - 25x^4 - 20x^3 - 10x^2 - 4x - 1$
   Phew—this one takes up a lot of page space. But it's not so complicated: Just multiply each term and then combine like terms.

6. $x^4 - 2x^2 - 2x - 1$

7. $10x^2 + 6x + 4$
   Hope you noticed the addition sign between these two, and then we hope you noticed the different signs between the terms.

8. $x^5 - 2x^4 + 1$

ANSWERS TO EXERCISE 5.2

1. $(x + 6)(x - 4)$
2. $(x - 2)(x - 1)$
3. $(x + 3)(x + 4)$
4. $(x + 5)^2$
5. $(x + 8)(x - 8)$
6. $(x - 7)^2$
7. $(4x + 3)^2$
8. $(3x + 4)(3x - 5)$

ANSWERS TO EXERCISE 5.3

1. $x = 3$ or 2

2. $x = 2\sqrt{3} - 2$ or $-2\sqrt{3} - 2$
   For this one you had to either complete the square or use the quadratic formula. Not too bad, was it?

3. $x = 7$ or -2

4. $x = \dfrac{1+\sqrt{13}}{3}$ or $\dfrac{1-\sqrt{13}}{3}$
   The quadratic equation was your best bet here, due to the unwieldy coefficient of the first term.

5. $x = \dfrac{1-\sqrt{5}}{2}$ or $\dfrac{1+\sqrt{5}}{2}$

6. $x = -2$ or $\dfrac{3}{5}$

7. $\dfrac{7}{5}$ or -2

8. $x = -2 - \sqrt{13}$ or $-2 + \sqrt{13}$

ANSWERS TO EXERCISE 5.4

1. $x - 1$

   You could have seen that this was factorable, or you could have gone through the whole process of dividing, noticing how important it is to make the sign appropriate to the product. Always check your dividing.

2. $3x + 15 + \dfrac{36}{x-3}$

   There was a remainder, very tricky but workable.

3. $2x - 2$

   Isn't it beautiful when they work out as easily as this?

4. $5x - 13 + \dfrac{31}{x+3}$

5. $3x^2 + 2x + 4 + \dfrac{3}{x-1}$

6. $x^2 + 6x + 72 + \dfrac{426}{x-6}$

   Long and drawn out, but if you just follow through with your long division and check your result by multiplying it out, you'll see that even though it is unfamiliar, it is workable.

7. $x - 8$

   You could factor or you could divide through the missing terms, either way you're in business.

8. $x - 4y + \dfrac{6y^2}{x+y}$

   Just treat the y's as you would any other terms and you'll have no problems, particularly if you check your answer by multiplying through when you've found it.

6

Inequalities

Now that you are familiar (dare we say comfortable?) with equations and the various ways of factoring, manipulating, and solving them, it is time to address those related beings, **inequalities**. An inequality expresses terms as greater than or less than other terms or expressions. The signs go as follows:

$x > y$ means x is greater than y. The larger part of the sign opens towards the larger value. Note that the variables may represent fractions, negative numbers—any real numbers whatsoever.

$x < y$ means x is less than y.

$x \geq y$ means x is greater than or equal to y, allowing for one more possibility than the usual $x > y$.

$x \leq y$ means x is less than or equal to y.

$x \neq y$ means x does not equal y, an inequality in the truest sense of the word.

PROPERTIES OF INEQUALITIES

Inequalities are less specific than equations, for instance, $x > 0$ means x is a positive number, but we don't have any more exact information as to which positive number. This presents something of a quandary: Sometimes linear or quadratic inequalities will be presented to you and you'll be expected to solve them, though you must remember that you will not be providing an exact solution. Solving an inequality in this manner requires that you proceed much as you would with an equation in which you were isolating the variable.

Let's try solving the following inequality.

$$2x + 3 > x - 1$$

The first step here is to combine like terms; then isolate x.

$2x + 3 > x - 1$ becomes $2x + 3 - x > x - 1 - x$
becomes $x + 3 > -1$ becomes $x > -4$

Thus, your solution is $x > -4$.

QUIRKS OF SOLVING INEQUALITIES

Due to the ways in which negative and positive numbers multiply with one another, you must be careful when isolating variables within inequalities that contain multiplications or divisions. For instance, you may be faced with an inequality such as this: $-2x > 4$.

To isolate the variable here you must divide both sides by -2. Dividing by -2 means changing the sign of the number on the right side of the equation, which means the direction of the greater-than sign will be affected.

> Here's the rule: When dividing or multiplying by a negative number in an inequality, you must reverse the direction of the inequality sign.

So, isolate x in the inequality discussed earlier.

$-2x > 4$ becomes $-\dfrac{1}{2}(-2x) < (4)-\dfrac{1}{2}$ becomes $x < -2$

Also, variables with exponents in inequalities may represent, as may any variable, negative numbers, so you must be careful when solving inequalities of the second degree or higher.

For instance, to isolate the variable in $x^2 > 4$, one must take the square root of both sides. Thus, $x > 2$ or $x < -2$.

EXERCISE 6.1

Solve all of the following inequalities.

1. $3x + 7 > 10$

2. $2x < x + 5$

3. $5a > -3$

4. $-6c < 3c + 2$

5. $-4x > 8$

6. $-\dfrac{x}{2} > -7$

7. $x^2 + 6x + 9 > 0$

8. $x^2 - x - 20 < 0$

ANSWERS TO CHAPTER SIX EXERCISES

ANSWERS TO EXERCISE 6.1

1. $x > 1$

2. $x < 5$

3. $a > -\dfrac{3}{5}$

4. $c > -\dfrac{2}{9}$

5. $x < -2$

6. $x < 14$

7. $x \neq -3$

    This one is a little unusual. You can't exactly say that $x > -3$ only, or $x < -3$ only, because it can be both. What the equation implies, rather, is that x cannot be -3 in particular, so the sign is more appropriate here than a greater than or less than sign.

8. $-4 < x < 5$

    Tricky, isn't it? Notice that if x were equal to anything outside of these boundaries the equation would be positive or equal to 0.

CHAPTER 7

Permutations, Combinations, and the Binomial Theorem

PERMUTATIONS AND COMBINATIONS

If there were five different insects—say an ant, a grasshopper, a beetle, a ladybug, and a mosquito—and you had to arrange them in a line, how many different insects could be first? Why, five of course, because you could choose any one of them to be first. Now, after you select one insect to be first, how many possible choices are left for the second place? Four, because there would be four insects left to arrange after having placed the first one. The next position has three possibilities, the one after that has two, and that leaves only one insect left for the final position, after the first four have been filled. So how many total possible arrangements exist?

$$5 \cdot 4 \cdot 3 \cdot 2 \cdot 1 = 120$$

There just happens to be a special name for "possible arrangements." This name is **permutation**; we have just looked at how many permutations there are for ordering five insects. The operation that calculates the number of permutations is called a **factorial**, and it's denoted by an exclamation point. A factorial is the product of a number and all of the whole numbers less than it, excluding zero. The way 5! is pronounced is "five factorial."

$$5! = 5 \cdot 4 \cdot 3 \cdot 2 \cdot 1 = 120$$
$$3! = 3 \cdot 2 \cdot 1 = 6$$

Why an exclamation point? Who knows, maybe there was a bit of giddiness running around the mathematical community in those days. At any rate, you pronounce 5! as "five factorial," not "Five! O! What a wonderful number!" or anything along those lines.

FIGURING OUT FACTORIALS

What do you think 0! might be? Well, how many ways are there to arrange nothing? One way, really, if you call leaving it as nothing an arrangement, which mathematicians, those sticklers, do. That is, more or less, the reason that 0! is always equal to 1. There is generally a factorial function on most calculators that is designated $x!$. The algebraic description of a factorial is $n! = n(n - 1)(n - 2)$ $(n - 3) \ldots 2 \cdot 1$. That means, as you can already see, that the factorial of a number is the product of that number and all the whole numbers less than it, excluding zero.

PERMUTATION NOTATION

The mathematical notation for a specific permutation looks like this: $P(n, n)$ in which n is the number of objects being arranged. To designate the permutations of an arrangement of five animals you could write $P(5, 5)$, $_5P_5$, or even $P\left(\frac{5}{5}\right)$, with or without the parentheses. Why do all of these have the number of objects in the permutation in two places? Read on.

PLAYING FAVORITES

Sometimes you'll have to calculate the permutations of a chosen number of items within a group. This would be the case if, for instance, you were arranging the insects again, but this time you were arranging only three of them out of the group of five. A smaller number of items to be arranged within the group of a larger number is designated as $P(n, k)$, in which n is the total number of objects in the group and k is the smaller number to be selected for an arrangement. So an arrangement of three out of five insects looks like this: $P(5, 3)$. How is it calculated? Well, how many possible insects are there for the first position? That's right, there are still 5 possible insects for the first position. There are 4 for the second position and

3 for the third position. So there are 5 · 4 · 3 total possibilities, or 60 total. How is this designated algebraically?

$$P(n,k) = \frac{n!}{(n-k)!}$$

In other words, the number of ways of choosing three out of five insects and arranging them in a specific order would look like this:

$$P(5,3) = \frac{5!}{(5-3)!}$$

This whole operation is described as a permutation of five objects taken three at a time, or more generally, as a permutation of n objects taken k at a time. As you perform the calculations for permutations, you'll see that it's unbelievably easy to cancel before multiplying anything, and at times canceling will eliminate the need to multiply at all.

CHAOS!

What if the order of the objects is irrelevant? What if you were supposed to find a combination of three insects out of five, but you didn't have to arrange them? In that case, you're only looking for the different combinations that can be selected, and you don't have to worry about who or what is first or second. Not surprisingly, an operation such as this is called a **combination**, and it's depicted in these ways: $C(n,k)$, ${}_nC_k$, or $\binom{n}{k}$. And what else do we call these $\binom{n}{k}$s? We call them **binomial coefficients**. Wouldn't you like to know why? Of course you would, but it will all be explained soon enough.

How do you calculate the number of combinations? It's a lot like the way you calculate the number of permutations, except that there are fewer possible combinations than permutations, because ant, grasshopper, mosquito and mosquito, grasshopper, ant are counted as one possible combination, where they would count as two different permutations because they are ordered differently.

$$C(n,k) = \binom{n}{k} = \frac{n!}{k!(n-k)!}$$

In these cases, as with permutations, you'll find it exceedingly easy to cancel from the top and bottom of the fraction.

Example

How many ways are there to select 4 students from a group of 6?

Clearly this is a combination problem, as the order or arrangement of the selected students is not an issue. Essentially the problem is asking: What is $\binom{6}{4}$? Put it into the formula, and you're there.

$$\frac{6!}{4!(6-4)!} = \frac{6 \cdot 5 \cdot 4 \cdot 3 \cdot 2}{4 \cdot 3 \cdot 2(2)}$$

Cancel where you can and you get 15. And that's how many ways there are to select 4 students from a group of 6.

EXERCISE 7.1

1. How many ways are there to arrange six books on a bookshelf?

2. How many different ways are there to select four of six books and order them on a bookshelf?

3. How many different ways are there to select three of six books and order them on a bookshelf?

4. How many different groups of two books can be selected from a group of six books?

5. How many possible different pairs can be selected from a group of eighteen people?

6. What is $P(7, 3)$?

7. What is $C(7, 3)$?

8. What is $C(5, 1)$?

THE BINOMIAL THEOREM

You've seen $(x + y)^2$ often enough by now to know that it is, in expanded form, $x^2 + 2xy + y^2$. And if you saw $(x + y)^3$ you would, without too much pain, be able to expand it out correctly to $x^3 + 3x^2 y + 3xy^2 + y^3$. But what if you saw $(x + y)^7$ or even $(x + y)^{27}$? How do you calculate the coefficients within the expanded expressions? As you can see from the squared and cubed examples here, the first and last terms of the expanded expression will always be the first and last terms of the original expression raised to the original exponent. But what about the coefficients in-between the first and last? For these, people used to rely on Pascal's Triangle, which looks like this:

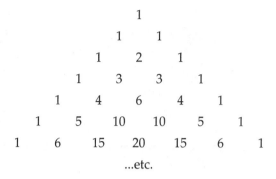

```
                1
             1     1
          1     2     1
       1     3     3     1
    1     4     6     4     1
 1     5    10    10     5     1
1   6    15    20    15    6    1
              ...etc.
```

Now, Pascal's Triangle is indeed brilliant and amazing. It gives the coefficients of the raised x and y terms for expressions raised to an infinite number of powers. For instance, the first term is for $(x + y)$ raised to the 0, which gives us 1. The second terms are for $(x + y)$ raised to the 1, which gives us $(x + y)$, both of which have coefficients of 1. You will recognize the next row of coefficients, 1, 2, and 1, as the coefficients of $(x + y)^2$ which expands to $x^2 + 2xy + y^2$. You might also notice that each of the numbers in the rows of Pascal's Triangle is the sum of the two numbers triangularly above it, or, if it is at the edge, just 1. This was a very brilliant thing for Pascal to do, but it is also a somewhat laborious method to use. We're here to tell you that there's another way in which any of these expansions can be calculated: by using the **binomial theorem**.

The binomial theorem can be expressed as

$$\left(x+y\right)^n = \binom{n}{0}x^n y^0 + \binom{n}{1}x^{n-1}y^1 + \binom{n}{2}x^{n-2}y^2 + \ldots + \binom{n}{n-1}x^1 y^{n-1} + \binom{n}{n}x^0 y^n$$

Ah! *That's* why combinations are also called binomial coefficients, because you can see that the coefficients of the binomial theorem are combinations! As for the exponents that apply to each term, you see that the sum of the first pair of exponents, n and 0, is n, which is also the sum of the last pair, 0 and n. You will notice (and we mean that; you will notice it if we have to come out there and make you notice it!) that the relationship between the x and y exponents follows this pattern through the series: $n - 1$ and 1, $n - 2$ and 2, and so on.

Now you can find the terms of any expansion, and a number of things might make determining the binomial coefficients even easier. One is that the function for calculating combinations is on most calculators in the form $_nC_r$, in which n is the overall number and r is the selected number. Another way to make life easier is obvious from the symmetry of Pascal's triangle. Is there any similarity between $\binom{9}{0}$ and $\binom{9}{9}$? Certainly, they give the same number. There is one way to select all nine out of a group, and one way to select none. But the symmetry doesn't stop there, it continues through all the possible combinations. For instance, $\binom{9}{1}$ and $\binom{9}{8}$: there are nine ways to select just one of nine, and nine ways to select eight of nine. You can look at it as $\binom{n}{k} = \binom{n}{n-k}$. A pretty nifty state of affairs.

Now try an expansion on your own, using the binomial theorem.

Example

What is the expansion of $(x + y)^7$?

Just rewrite it in the binomial formula and calculate the combinations.

$$(x+y)^7 = \binom{7}{0}x^7y^0 + \binom{7}{1}x^6y^1 + \binom{7}{2}x^5y^2 + \binom{7}{3}x^4y^3$$
$$+ \binom{7}{4}x^3y^4 + \binom{7}{5}x^2y^5 + \binom{7}{6}x^1y^6 + \binom{7}{7}x^0y^7$$

This becomes:

$$x^7 + 7x^6y + 21x^5y^2 + 35x^4y^3 + 35x^3y^4 + 21x^2y^5 + 7x^1y^6 + y^7$$

Which happens to be your answer.

PROVING THE BINOMIAL THEOREM

To prove the binomial theorem, we must turn to a process called the principle of mathematical induction. Mathematical induction says that in order to prove that something is true for all positive integers n, you must prove that it is true for $n = 1$; in addition, you must prove that if it is true for $n = k$, it is also true for $n = k + 1$.

You can see why these are necessities if you consider that you want the statement to hold true through infinity.

As for proving the binomial theorem, you've already seen that $(x + y)^1 = \binom{1}{0}x^1y^0 + \binom{1}{1}x^0y^1$ works with the theorem, so the first principle of mathematical induction, when $n = 1$, is taken care of. When $n = k$, well, you've already seen the theorem worked out for a positive integer k. Now how do you show that it will work as well for $k + 1$? Start with the binomial expansion for $(x + y)^k$. How many factors will that be? Well, there are k groups of $(x + y)$. We know what this looks like when it's expressed by the binomial theorem.

$$(x+y)^k = \binom{k}{0}x^k y^0 + \binom{k}{1}x^{k-1}y^1 + \binom{k}{2}x^{k-2}y^2 + \ldots + \binom{k}{k}x^0 y^k$$

Now, to see if this will work for $k + 1$, multiply both sides of the equation by $(x + y)$. This will give you $k + 1$ factors, instead of k factors of $(x + y)$. You perform this operation just as you would if you were multiplying polynomials, by multiplying by each term within the parentheses and then stacking them.

The left side becomes

$$(x + y)^k(x + y), \text{ or } (x + y)^{k+1}$$

The right side is expressed as follows: The top stack is all of the terms in the expansion multiplied by x, the bottom is the expansion multiplied by y. Notice that to make the process clearer, we included the second-to-last term of the bottom stack in place of the third term.

$$\binom{k}{0}x^k y^0(x) + \binom{k}{1}x^{k-1}y^1(x) + \binom{k}{2}x^{k-2}y^2(x) + \ldots + \binom{k}{k}x^0 y^k(x)$$

$$+ \left[\binom{k}{0}x^k y^0(y) + \binom{k}{1}x^{k-1}y^1(y) + \ldots + \binom{k}{k-1}x^1 y^{k-1}(y) + \binom{k}{k}x^0 y^k(y)\right]$$

This can be rewritten by combining the exponents, and then aligning like terms, as

$$\binom{k}{0}x^{k+1}y^0 + \binom{k}{1}x^k y^1 + \binom{k}{2}x^{k-1}y^2 + \ldots + \binom{k}{k}x^1 y^k$$

$$+ \quad \binom{k}{0}x^k y^1 + \binom{k}{1}x^{k-1}y^2 + \ldots + \binom{k}{k-1}x^1 y^k + \binom{k}{k}x^0 y^{k+1}$$

$$\overline{\binom{k}{0}x^{k+1}y^0 + \left[\binom{k}{1}+\binom{k}{0}\right]x^k y^1 + \left[\binom{k}{2}+\binom{k}{1}\right]x^{k-1}y^2 + \ldots + \left[\binom{k}{k-1}+\binom{k}{k}\right]x^1 y^k + \binom{k}{k}x^0 y^{k+1}}$$

As you can see, the beginning and end of this sum look all right; you can basically think of the first term as x^{k+1} and the last term as y^{k+1}. But how do you know that these coefficients are the real McCoy? What you want is for the sum of the coefficients, the $\binom{k}{1}$ plus the $\binom{k}{0}$ on the second term, for instance, to be the appropriate coefficient for that second term according to the binomial theorem. Since the second term is $x^k y^1$, the binomial coefficient should be $\binom{k+1}{1}$.

So here comes the second part of the proof: Is $\binom{k}{n}+\binom{k}{n-1}=\binom{k+1}{n}$? Once we show that it is, we're sitting pretty. We must then go ahead and add them, and see if we get the right side of the equation.

$$\binom{k}{n} + \binom{k}{n-1} = \frac{k!}{n!(k-n)!} + \frac{k!}{(n-1)!(k-[n-1])!}$$

Let's first simplify:

$$\frac{k!}{n!(k-n)!} + \frac{k!}{(n-1)!(k-[n-1])!} = \frac{k!}{n!(k-n)!} + \frac{k!}{(n-1)!(k-n+1)!}$$

Now before adding the fractions, let's make them have the same denominator, which is easier than it looks. Really, to make $(k-n)!$ into $(k-n+1)!$ is not too complex when you remember what a factorial is.

$$\frac{k!}{n!(k-n)!} \cdot \left(\frac{k-n+1}{k-n+1}\right) = \frac{k!(k-n+1)}{n!(k-n+1)!}$$

And to make $(n-1)!$ into $n!$ is quite similar—just remember what a factorial is.

$$\frac{k!}{(n-1)!(k-n+1)!} \cdot \left(\frac{n}{n}\right) = \frac{k!n}{n!(k-n+1)!}$$

Now, add them.

$$\frac{k!(k-n+1)}{n!(k-n+1)!} + \frac{k!n}{n!(k-n+1)!} = \frac{k!(k-n+1)+k!n}{n!(k-n+1)!}$$

You can factor the top.

$$\frac{k!(k-n+1+n)}{n!(k-n+1)!} \text{ becomes } \frac{k!(k+1)}{n!(k-n+1)!}$$

Now you can see that the top is really another way of saying $(k+1)!$.

$$\frac{(k+1)!}{n!(k-n+1)!}$$

It might look a little spooky until you realize exactly what you are looking at, because $\dfrac{(k+1)!}{n!(k-n+1)!}$ also happens to be a very nice representation of $\binom{k+1}{n}$. And the binomial theorem is proved.

FUNKY LITTLE THINGS THAT MIGHT COME UP

What if you have a binomial that isn't sweet and tractable like $(x + y)$ but is creepy and frightening like $(2a - b^2)$? No sweat, just use $2a$ as your x and b^2 as your y, and base your expansion on these two and whatever exponent you are given. It's a piece of cake.

ANSWERS TO CHAPTER SEVEN EXERCISE

EXERCISE 7.1

1. 720
2. 360
3. 120
4. 15
5. 153
6. 210
7. 35
8. 5

Geometry

Geometry is the study of the measurements and relationships between shapes. We'll start with **plane geometry**, the geometry of flat or two-dimensional figures. You're familiar with the shapes we're about to cover (you've probably doodled them compulsively for years), but after this you're going to know more about them than ever before.

PROOFS

Many of the geometry questions you'll encounter here and elsewhere will ask you to prove facts about one particular shape or another. What these questions are asking you for, technically, are proofs. Proofs aren't any big mystery; they want exactly what the name says. However, they want a specific level of detail that you might not ordinarily feel compelled to give. For instance, here we will ask you to show how and why certain things are true. What we are really asking you to do is to prove them. In most geometry classes (and on some tests as well) you will be asked to *prove* even the most obvious-seeming facts by way of axioms and postulates.

These "givens" include rules you will encounter in the upcoming sections, such as the rule of 180 on page 96, and the corresponding inscribed angles in a circle rule of page 113, and even the rule that two parallel lines will never meet. The way that proofs are different from general questions that ask you to show that something is true is that proofs ask you to cite each particular applicable rule as you go through the process.

Proofs can be a wonderful exercise in clarifying the thought process involved in solving problems, but make no mistake, a clear understanding of that information can yield further information; and that's the most important thing. Getting further pieces of information from one piece of information is called deduction, and deduction helps you get from what appears to be true to an understanding of whether it is, indeed, true and why that is. We do not review proofs here per se; we want you to understand the nature of proofs and why they are used, and to understand the shapes and forms with which proofs are concerned. Thus, after going through the exercises and the information here, we hope you will go on to your class geometry assignments armed with an understanding of why you are asked to provide proofs, and of the workings of the shapes and properties you are asked to provide proofs about.

8

Plane Geometry

The basic units of plane geometry are **points** and **lines**. Lines continue in both directions to infinity. They are made up of an infinite number of points, each of which occupies a particular space on the line. Lines can be straight, curved, or even broken; for now we will discuss straight lines only.

The unit of measurement that is generally used for lines and angles in plane geometry is the **degree**. A straight line measures 180 degrees.

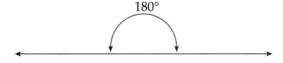

180°

The "lines" one normally refers to are actually **line segments**, which are cut-up pieces of lines.

Why is this section called plane geometry? Because all of the geometry we'll be talking about occurs in a **plane**. A plane is a two-dimensional space extending infinitely in all directions. Think of a piece of paper that extends, top and bottom, both sides, forever. Then imagine that the paper has no measurable thickness; really cheap, thin paper, for instance. That's a good way to imagine what a plane is.

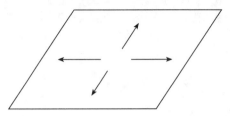

When we say that geometry occurs in a plane, we mean that these shapes and lines are flat; they exist only on the planar level.

SPECIAL LINES

Parallel lines are lines that maintain the same distance between them infinitely, and never meet.

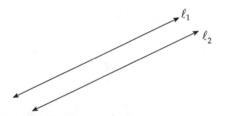

The mathematical symbol for parallel lines is two straight lines between the variable for the lines; for example $l_1 \parallel l_2$ is "line one is parallel to line two."

ANGLES

Lines that *aren't* parallel end up meeting eventually. When two lines meet they form four **angles**.

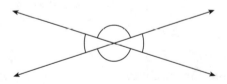

Angles opposite one another are called **vertical angles**, and vertical angles are always equal, meaning they have the same degree measure. The way to mark equal angles is to stick a line into the angle curves; equal angles or sides have the same number of lines through them, like so:

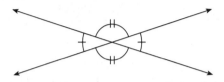

Angles that cut the degree measure of a line in half are said to be perpendicular, and are denoted by a small square in the vertex of the angle.

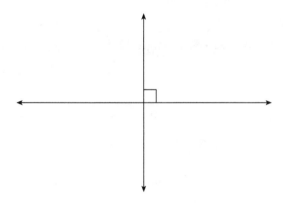

Since the 180° line is cut exactly in half, perpendicular angles measure exactly 90 degrees.

Two angles that together add up to the measure of a line, or 180 degrees, are called **supplementary**. Two **complementary** angles add up to form a perpendicular, or 90 degrees.

SOME THINGS TO KNOW ABOUT LINES AND ANGLES

If two parallel lines are intersected by a third line, the **alternate interior** angles formed by that third line are equal, and the corresponding angles—you can see that these are the vertical angles of the alternate interior angles—are also equal. This is called the **rule of alternate interior angles**. Remember, angles that are exactly the same size are marked with equal numbers of lines through them.

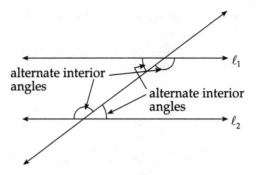

An angle greater than 90 degrees is referred to as **obtuse**. An angle less than 90 degrees is called **acute**.

Now make sure you're comfortable with the information we've given thus far.

EXERCISE 8.1

1. How many degrees is angle *b*?

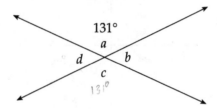

2. How many degrees is angle *c*?

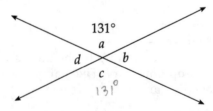

3. Which of the angles is the vertical angle of angle *g*?

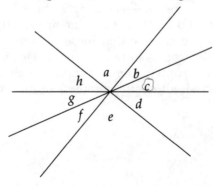

4. Is angle *d* supplementary to angle *e*, complementary, or neither?

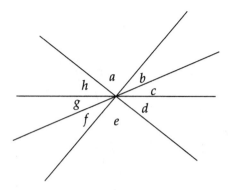

5. Does angle *f* measure the same as angle *b*, *d*, *e*, or *a*?

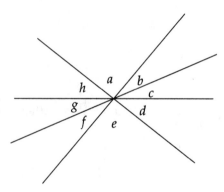

6. Which angle pairs measure 180° here?

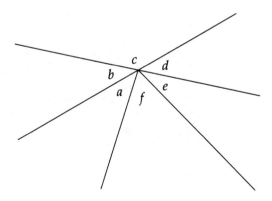

7. If l_1 and l_2 are parallel, what is the measure of angle a? What other angles are equal to angle a?

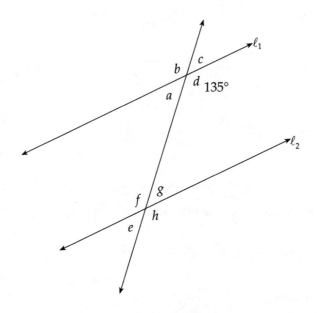

8. How many degrees is angle f? What other angles are equal to angle f?

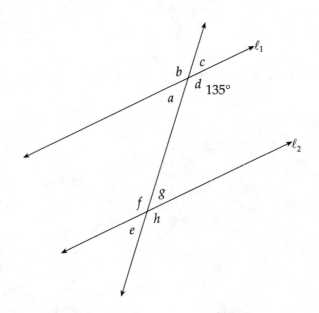

QUADRILATERALS

A **quadrilateral** is a closed, two-dimensional shape that has four sides. Closed means that the four sides meet at the corners rather then opening up, like this:

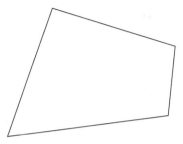

rather than this:

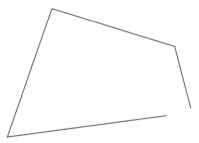

The sum of the degrees of the four internal angles in a quadrilateral is 360. Quadrilaterals are divided into groups according to their more specific properties.

To find the **area** of a quadrilateral, multiply its **base** times its **height**. Its area is defined as the number of square units the shape occupies.

Area of a quadrilateral = bh

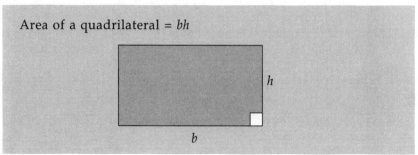

The height of any shape is the vertical distance of a perpendicular line drawn from the highest point of the quadrilateral to its base.

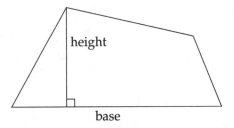

base

To find the **perimeter** of a quadrilateral or any other shape, add up the sides. The perimeter is the distance around the outside of a shape. When you have a quadrilateral with two pairs of equal sides, you can find the perimeter by multiplying the length by two, multiplying the width by two, and adding these. This is, of course, the same as adding all four sides.

TRIANGLES

When you split a quadrilateral diagonally things really start to happen, because you've created two triangles.

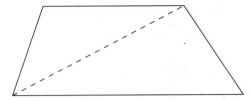

Triangles are three-sided figures. Since two triangles account for one quadrilateral, what do one triangle's angles add up to? You've got it, half of the degrees of a quadrilateral, which is half of 360—in other words, the sum of the internal angles of a triangle is 180 degrees. This is called the **rule of 180**. Now, since a triangle is essentially half of a quadrilateral, what is the area of a triangle? Half of the area of a quadrilateral, or one-half the base times the height.

$$\text{Area of a triangle} = \frac{1}{2}bh$$

The angles of a triangle are directly proportional to the sides opposite them; in other words, the largest angle is always opposite the longest side, and the smallest angle is always opposite the shortest side. When all of the sides of a triangle are equal, all of its angles are equal. A triangle of this type is an **equilateral triangle**.

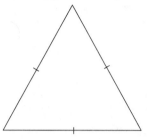

If all of its angles are equal, what is the measure of each angle? Why, 60 degrees of course, because the sum of the angles must be 180°.

If a triangle has two sides that are exactly equal, then the angles opposite those two sides are also equal. A triangle with two equal sides is an **isosceles triangle**.

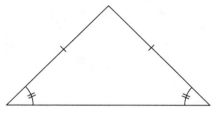

Any **exterior** angle of a triangle is equal to the sum of the two opposite **interior** angles, no matter what type of triangle it is. An exterior angle is an angle abutting but outside the shape; an interior angle is inside the shape. Can you see why this is true (think about the rule of 180°)?

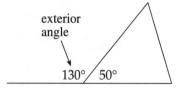

exterior angle

130° / 50°

interior angles

103° / 77°

RIGHT TRIANGLES

A triangle that contains a right angle is a **right triangle**.

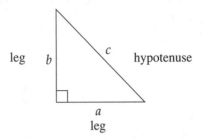

The side opposite the right angle is called the **hypotenuse**, and the other sides of the triangle are called **legs**. The relationship between the length of the legs and the length of the hypotenuse of a right triangle is as follows: $a^2 + b^2 = c^2$, in which c is the hypotenuse and a and b are the legs of the right triangle. This is known as the **Pythagorean Theorem**; you will grow to love and admire it when its many fabulous applications become apparent to you.

Two types of right triangles, the isosceles right triangle and the 30: 60: 90 right triangle, have specific numerical ratios among their sides. For the isosceles right triangle, where the legs of the triangle are x, the hypotenuse is $x\sqrt{2}$.

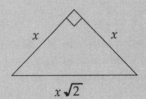

For the 30: 60: 90 right triangle, the shortest leg is x, the middle leg is $x\sqrt{3}$, and the longest leg is $2x$.

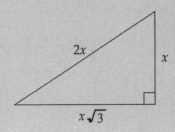

Example

What is the area of the rectangle $ABCD$?

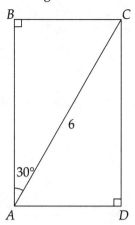

To find the area of the rectangle, the information that's already there needs to be evaluated. Note that by providing the diagonal of the rectangle, the diagram also shows that there are two equal right triangles. Why equal? Well, they share a hypotenuse, they have equal bases and heights, and they have equal angles, because the thirty degree angle shown has a complementary angle of 60 degrees, which means that the angles opposite them are also 60 degrees and 30 degrees.

To find the area of a rectangle, what information is necessary? The base and the height. How can we find the base and the height? Well, the base and the height of the rectangle happen to be equal to the base and the height of these right triangles. By noting that they are 30:60:90 right triangles, which have a specific ratio of side lengths of $x : x\sqrt{3} : 2x$, we can determine all three sides just by finding the measure of one. Do we have the measure of any of these sides? Yes, we have the measure of the hypotenuse, 6. The hypotenuse corresponds to the largest of the edges on the ratio, $2x$. If $2x = 6$, then $x = 3$. Thus, the remaining sides of x and $x\sqrt{3}$ are 3 and $3\sqrt{3}$ respectively.

The area of a rectangle is *bh*, so the area of this rectangle is 3 times $3\sqrt{3}$, or $9\sqrt{3}$.

That's an awful lot of triangle information to review; go through this next exercise and see how comfortable you are with it before moving on.

EXERCISE 8.2

1. What is the area of a triangle with a base of 2 and a height of 4?

2. What is the measure of angle *b*?

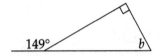

3. What is the height of triangle *ABC*?

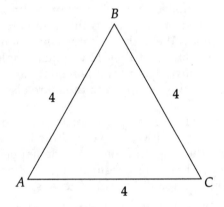

4. What is the area of triangle *ABC* above?

5. What is the measure of angle *x*?

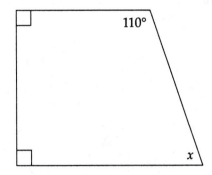

6. In the figure, find the measure of angles *a*, *b*, *d*, and *e*.

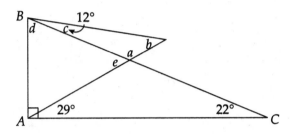

7. What is the length of side *a* in terms of *x*?

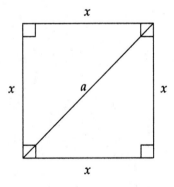

8. Equilateral triangle *ABC* has a side that forms the height of equilateral triangle *DBE*. What is the ratio of the areas of these two triangles?

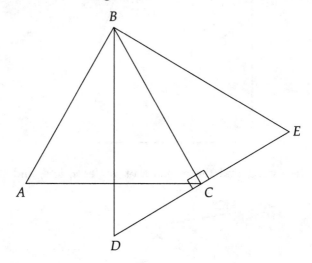

SIMILAR TRIANGLES

Any two (or more) triangles are similar if their corresponding angles are equal. This is because equal angles imply the same shape; thus, these triangles' sides are proportional.

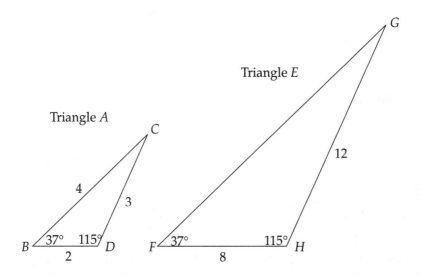

Similar triangles allow you to determine missing information by providing the ratio of the sides. For example, look at triangle A and triangle E. You can tell they're similar because of their equal angles (angle FGH must be 28° because of the rule of 180). You can also tell that their ratio is such that the sides of triangle E are four times the sides of triangle A. This is determined from the ratio of side BD to side FH. Thus, you can determine side FG in triangle E; it must be four times the respective side of triangle A, or 16.

AREA OF SIMILAR TRIANGLES

How is the area of two pairs of similar triangles proportional? Well, take a look at the triangles again.

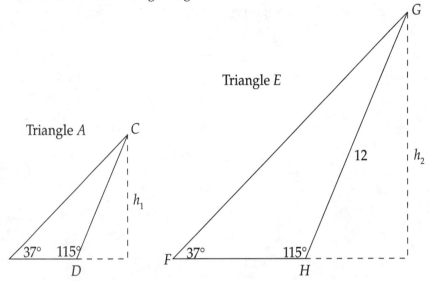

The sides are proportional, which means that they all have the same ratio. Another way of expressing this is $\frac{BD}{FH} = \frac{BD}{FG} = \frac{CD}{DH}$. Since these sides are proportional, you know that the heights are proportional, or $\frac{h_1}{h_2}$.

The area of triangle A is $(BD)(h_1)\left(\frac{1}{2}\right)$. The area of triangle E is $(FH)(h_2)\left(\frac{1}{2}\right)$, so the proportion of the areas is $\dfrac{(BD)(h_1)\left(\frac{1}{2}\right)}{(FH)(h_2)\left(\frac{1}{2}\right)}$. Thankfully, you can simplify this fraction. The halves cancel out, and you have $\frac{(BD)(h_1)}{(FH)(h_2)}$, which can also be seen as $\left(\frac{BD}{FH}\right)\left(\frac{h_1}{h_2}\right)$. Of course, since the sides and the heights have the same proportion, you could also write this as $\left(\frac{BD}{FH}\right)\left(\frac{BD}{FH}\right)$ or better yet, as $\left(\frac{BD}{FH}\right)^2$. All of which goes to show you that the ratio of the areas of two similar triangles is equal to the square of the ratios of their sides.

CONGRUENCE

Triangles that are exactly the same size are **congruent**. This term also applies to angles of the same measure, which we've already seen in isosceles, equilateral, and similar triangles. (Remember?) In an equation, the symbol for congruence is ≅, as in, angle $ABC \cong$ angle EGH.

EXERCISE 8.3

1. What is the measure of x if the broken line is parallel to the base?

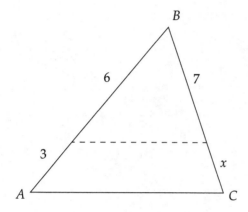

2. Express the area of triangle *RSY* algebraically.

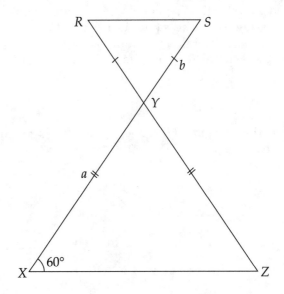

3. What is the ratio of the area of *RSY* to the area of *XYZ*?

4. What is *x*?

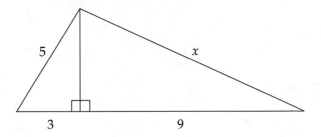

5. What is the distance of *JM*?

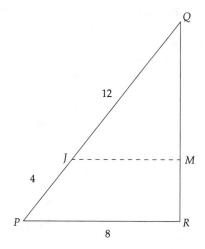

6. What is the distance of *MR* in the triangle above?

7. Given the information in the diagram, show that the triangle is isosceles.

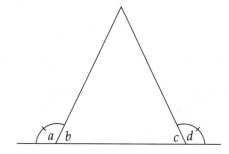

8. What is the area of triangle *DBE*?

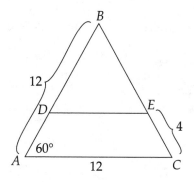

CIRCLES

A round figure in which all points on the outside perimeter are equidistant from the point in the center is called a **circle**. The point in the middle of a circle is called the **center**, and any line that passes through the center from one side of the circle to the other is a **diameter**. A line that extends from the center of a circle to an edge is called a **radius**, and since that distance is equal all the way around the edge of a circle, all radii (the plural of radius) of a circle are equal. For the same reason, all of the diameters of a circle are the same.

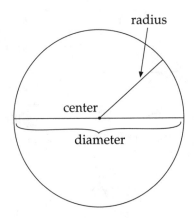

The measurement around the edge of a circle is called the **circumference** (it's called the perimeter for other shapes). All circles are similar in that they all have the same proportions, just like similar triangles. The most important of these proportions is the ratio of a circle's circumference to its diameter; this ratio is always 3.1415927...or approximately 3.14; in fraction form it is approximately $\frac{22}{7}$. This irrational, non-repeating decimal is known as **pi**, the Greek letter π. Pi is extremely important in all circle calculations. Since π expresses the ratio of the circumference to the diameter, the formula for the circumference of a circle is $c = \pi d$, in which c is the circumference and d is the diameter. This is often also depicted as $c = 2\pi r$, because the diameter is always equal to two times the radius. This second formula is sometimes easier to use because many algebraic equations refer to the radius. The area of a circle is expressed as $A = \pi r^2$, in which A is the area of a circle and r is the radius.

EXAMPLE

What is the area of a circle with a diameter of 16?

A circle's area is found by using the formula πr^2. At this point, what ingredient are you missing? To find the radius, divide the diameter by two. In this case, the diameter is 16, and half of 16 is 8. So the formula will read area = $\pi 8^2$ or, the area is equal to 64π.

SECTIONS OF CIRCLES

A line from one edge of the circle to another that does not go through the center is called a **chord**. Sections of a circle's actual circumference are called **arcs**. Arcs can be specified by three points along a circle's edge. Arcs of less than 180 degrees are called **minor arcs**.

The length of an arc is proportional to the arc's angle measure. For example, arc *ABD* in the circle below is opposite an angle of 30 degrees.

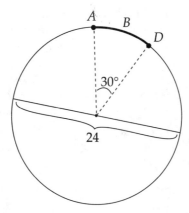

This means that the arc is $\frac{30}{360}$, or $\frac{1}{12}$ of the overall circumference, because the total circle is 360°, and the arc's angle is 30°. Since the diameter is 24, the circumference is 24π, and the length of the arc is one-twelfth of that, or 2π.

The surface measure of an arc is called a **sector**.

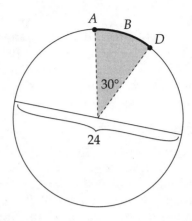

Again, the proportion of the arc to the whole circle is helpful in determining the measure of the area of a sector. Since the diameter of this circle is 24, the radius is 12, so the area is 144π. The 30 degree sector is still one-twelfth of the circle, so the area of the sector is one-twelfth of 144π, or 12π.

Area of a sector. Is there a formula, and if so, how would you derive it? Well, another way of looking at the proportion is to put the area of the sector, or A_s, over the area of the circle like so: $\dfrac{A_s}{\pi r^2}$. This is the same proportion as the length of the arc over the circumference of the circle, or $\dfrac{s}{2\pi r}$. So, $\dfrac{A_s}{\pi r^2} = \dfrac{s}{2\pi r}$.

To isolate A_s, multiply both sides by πr^2 to get $A_s = \dfrac{s}{2\pi r} \cdot \pi r^2$.

This becomes $A_s = \dfrac{sr}{2}$, or the length of the arc times the radius, times one-half. And that's the formula for the area of a sector. Do you recognize any similarity to any other area formula, like maybe the one for the area of a triangle?

Of course you can use this information backwards, too. If you're given the length of an arc and the measure of a circle's circumference, you can determine the angle because the proportion is given. For instance, in a circle with circumference 6π, an arc of length π would represent one-sixth of the circle, and thus have an angle measure of one-sixth of the 360 degree circle, or 60 degrees.

Example

What is the area of a sector of an angle of 20 degrees in a circle of circumference 36π?

Here you can use the formula for the area of a sector, which is $A_s = \dfrac{sr}{2}$. You need to find s, or the length of the sector (the arc part), to use the formula. You know that the sector is opposite a 20 degree angle, so the length is $\dfrac{20}{360}$, or one-eighteenth of the total length of the circle. What is the length of a circle? Its circumference; in this case, 36π. Therefore, the length of the arc is one-eighteenth times 36π, or 2π. What else do you need in the formula? The radius. Since you know the circumference is π times the diameter, you know that 36 gives you a diameter of 36π, and a radius of 18. Your formula is thus $\dfrac{2\pi 18}{2}$ which becomes 18π.

Another way to find the area is to find the ratio $\dfrac{1}{18}$ from the degree measure of the sector. Since the radius is still 18, the area of the circle is $\pi 18^2$, and you can see that the area of the sector is just one-eighteenth of the total area of the circle. They are, essentially, the same operation, and they give you the same area measure of your sector, 18π. It's just a question of how you'd like to work through the problem.

INSCRIBING

People just love to place shapes inside circles. Putting a shape inside a circle so that the vertices and ends of the non-circular shape touch the inside edge of the circle is called **inscribing**.

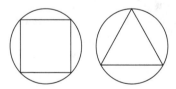

Shapes and angles can be inscribed in semicircles as well. Again, the vertices and ends of the shape or angle must touch the edge of the semicircle. An angle inscribed in a semicircle is, by definition, a right angle. All of the following angles are inscribed in a semicircle, thus they are all right angles.

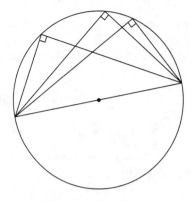

But the following angle is not inscribed in a semicircle; it's merely inside a semicircle, because all of its end points don't touch the edge of the semicircle.

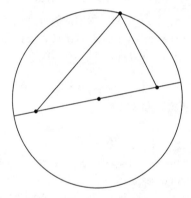

Since any angle inscribed in a semicircle is a right angle, any triangle inscribed in a semicircle is a right triangle.

INSCRIBED AND CORRESPONDING ANGLES

Angles inscribed in a semicircle are right angles due to a very cool property. An angle inscribed in a circle measures half of the angle formed by taking the ends of the original and joining them at the center.

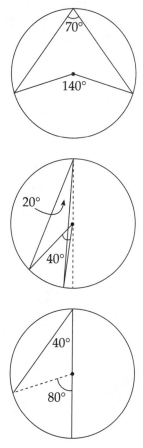

The angle formed by drawing these two new lines is called the **corresponding** angle of the inscribed angle.

The reason that this is true can be easily determined from the last figure. The angle created by the lines drawn from the end points of the first angle through the center of the circle—also called the corresponding angle—forms the exterior angle to a triangle, and thus must equal the sum of the opposite interior angles (remember this information from page 97?). Since the triangle here is an isosceles triangle (because two of its sides are radii), the two opposite interior angles are equal; one of them is the original angle we discussed. Thus, this interior angle is one-half of the measure of the exterior angle.

Since a triangle formed from two lines drawn from the center to the edge will always be formed of two radii, you will always be dealing with an isosceles triangle of one sort or another. Take a look at what these triangles look like drawn in on the other figures; note that in the first circle *two* isosceles triangles are formed.

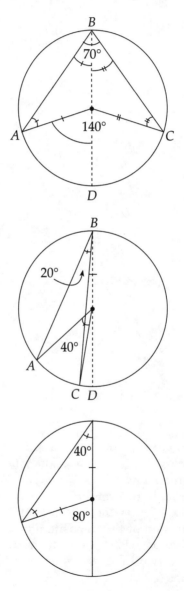

Example

What is the area of triangle *CDE* inscribed in a circle *C*, if diameter *FG* equals 12?

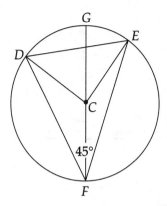

   To find the area of the triangle we must know its base and its height. So we must determine which dimensions of the triangle we already have. Since the diameter of the circle is 12, the radius is 6. Happily, two of our triangle's sides are radii. This does not necessarily mean that we know the height of the triangle in question, though. To find the height we need a perpendicular. Look at the triangle to see what information it contains, and what the measure of angle *ECD* is. Since it's the corresponding central angle of the inscribed angle, it must be twice the inscribed angle's measure, or twice 45, which is 90 degrees. Aha! Our corresponding angle is a right angle, meaning we've got a right isosceles triangle on our hands; the two sides formed by the radii are the height and the base because of the right angle. So the area of the triangle is $\frac{1}{2}(6 \cdot 6)$, or $\frac{1}{2}(36)$, or 18.

EXERCISE 8.4

1. Triangle *ABC* is inscribed in the semicircle *ABC*. What is the area of triangle *ABC*?

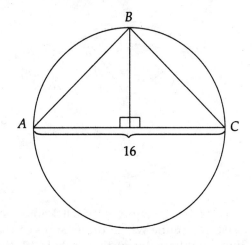

2. What is the area of semicircle *ABC*?

3. What is the area of triangle *FGH* in the circle with center *F*?

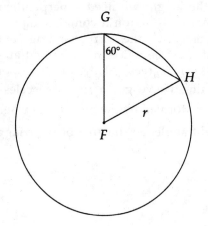

4. What is the area of the shaded portion of this figure?

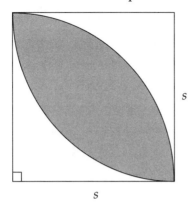

s

s

5. What is the area of the outer shaded ring?

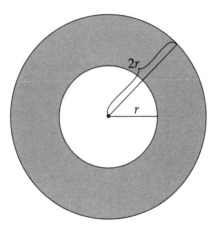

$2r$

r

6. What is the area of the shaded region?

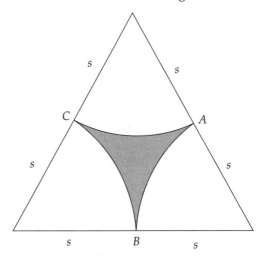

7. What is the ratio of the area of circle B to the area of circle with center A?

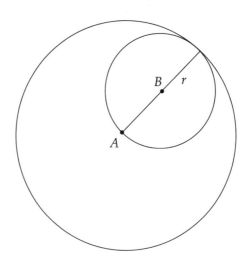

8. What is the area of a square inscribed in a circle of radius $2\sqrt{2}$?

ANSWERS TO CHAPTER EIGHT EXERCISES

ANSWERS TO EXERCISE 8.1

1. 49°
2. 131°
3. angle c
4. neither
5. angle b
6. d and c, and b and c
7. angle a is 45° and so are angles c, e, and g
8. angle f is 135° and so are angles h, b, and d

ANSWERS TO EXERCISE 8.2

1. 4
2. 59°
3. $2\sqrt{3}$
4. $4\sqrt{3}$
5. 70°
   (Draw in the line to make the other shape a rectangle and use the rule of 180 on the created triangle.)
6. Angle a is 129° (vertical from the triangle), so angle b is 39°. Angle e is supplementary to angle a, and is 51°. Angle d can be found by subtracting the 29 from the right angle to find the other angle in the triangle, and then using the rule of 180°; angle d is 68°.
7. $x\sqrt{2}$
8. $\dfrac{3}{4}$

ANSWERS TO EXERCISE 8.3

1. 3.5
   (Similar triangles, and don't forget to subtract out the 7.)

2. $\dfrac{b^2\sqrt{3}}{4}$

3. $\dfrac{b^2}{a^2}$

4. $\sqrt{97}$
   Use the Pythagorean Theorem to find the middle leg of the triangle on the left, and then to find the hypotenuse of the triangle on the right.

5. 6
   Similar triangles.

6. $2\sqrt{3}$
   With similar triangles and the Pythagorean Theorem you're pretty powerful.

7. The angles a and d are equal, which means that $180 - a = 180 - d$, and since $b = 180 - a$ and $c = 180 - d$, b and c are equal, which is the definition of an isosceles triangle.

8. $16\sqrt{3}$

ANSWERS TO EXERCISE 8.4

1. 32
   (the height is a radius)

2. 32π
   (half the area of the circle)

3. $\dfrac{r^2\sqrt{3}}{4}$

4. $s^2\left(\dfrac{\pi}{2}-1\right)$

You can find the area of each crescent-shaped, unshaded region by subtracting the area of a quarter-circle of radius s from the area of the square with edge s. If you then subtract two of these unshaded shapes from the area of the square, you're left with the shaded area indicated.

5. $3\pi r^2$

6. $\dfrac{s^2\left(\sqrt{3}-\pi\right)}{2}$

Each rounded corner of the triangle is one-sixth of a circle of radius s because they have angles of 60 degrees, being the vertices of an equilateral triangle. Thus all three add up to one-half of a circle; subtract that from the area of the triangle (the height is found by noting that it's the middle length leg of a 30 : 60 : 90 triangle), and you have the area of the shaded region.

7. $\dfrac{1}{4}$

8. 16

The diagonal of the circle forms the diagonal of the square. This divides the square into two isosceles right triangles, which have sides in a ratio of $x : x : x\sqrt{2}$. Since you have the hypotenuse, you can determine the side and then the area.

Solid Geometry

SOLID SHAPES

As you well know (you solid thing, you), life does not exist solely in a two-dimensional space. So it is for geometric shapes. There are those that exist in a two-dimensional plane that you just studied, and those that exist in space; three-dimensional or solid shapes. You're familiar with these shapes on the whole; they are extensions of the ones you encountered in plane geometry. For instance, a square extended by an edge of equal length along a third dimension is a **cube**.

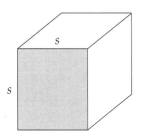

A square or rectangle extends to form a rectangular solid, also known as a **rectangular prism**. A circle in three dimensions so that every point on the outside surface is equidistant from the center is a sphere. An isosceles triangle turned around on its central axis forms a **cone**.

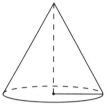

A circle lengthened through space forms a **cylinder**.

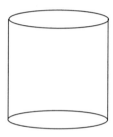

VOLUME

One of the important measures of a three-dimensional shape is its **volume**, which measures the three-dimensional space that it fills. While area is a measure of square units, volume is a measure of cubic units. Essentially all of the formulas for the volume of a three-dimensional figure are the same: Find the area of a two-dimensional surface of the shape, and then multiply this area by the third dimension. For instance, the volume of our base unit itself, the cube. The area of one **face** of the cube, which is just an ordinary square, is s^2.

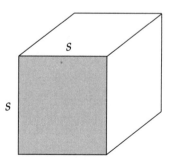

To find the volume, multiply this area by the third or additional dimension that makes it a cube (the third edge), which is also s. So, $s^2 \cdot s = s^3$. The volume of a cube is s^3.

The same principle applies to the rectangular solid.

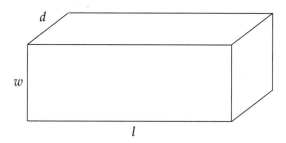

The area of this rectangle is lw. To find the volume of the solid then, multiply lw by the additional dimension, in this case, depth or d. So the volume of a rectangular solid is lwd.

For a cylinder, the area of the base is πr^2. The additional dimension is the height of the cylinder, and that's just what you multiply by to find the volume. The volume of a cylinder is $\pi r^2 h$.

The volume of a triangular prism is the area of one face times the third dimension, just as it is in other elongated shapes.

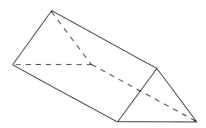

Another way of expressing it is bh, in which b is the area of the triangular base, or $\frac{1}{2}bh$.

The volume of triangular-based pyramids, cones, and spheres are a bit less easily explained. We provide the formulas here; ideas about how the formulas are derived follow in the box below.

The volume of a triangular-based pyramid is $\frac{1}{3}Bh$, the volume of a cone is $\frac{1}{3}\pi r^2 h$, and the volume of a sphere is $\frac{4}{3}\pi r^3$.

How does one find the volume of these shapes? Start with finding the volume of a pyramid with a triangular base. We can do this by taking a shape we know—the triangular prism—and slicing it up to form three pyramids with triangular bases. (Try this with a piece of clay if you happen to have one lying around.) Since the triangular-based pyramids are equal thirds, the volumes are equal thirds of the volume of a triangular prism, or each pyramid formed has a volume of $\frac{1}{3}Bh$. On to the cone.

A cone's relationship to the cylinder is numerically the same as that of the triangular-based pyramid to the triangular prism, so $\frac{1}{3}\pi r^2 h$ as the area of a cone makes a lot of sense. To prove it? Well, that's related to something else; it's related to another form of proof in which the volume formulas for shapes are found by recognizing their equivalence to shapes of the same volume but different compositions. For instance, the volume of a sphere is found by imagining the sphere as a large number of equally thick disks, sliced up sort of like a hard-boiled egg.

There's a lot more to this process of finding volumes of three-dimensional objects, but it will have to wait until you have a stronger grasp on various number and function principles. For now, be content to know the formulas and have some inkling of how they are derived. You may already have a better idea of how it all works if you figured out that a sphere doesn't have a height as a dimension to multiply by, just another radius, so the r^3 ends up representing the three-dimensionality of the thing.

SURFACE AREA

Another measure of three-dimensional shapes is **surface area**. Surface area represents the entire exterior surface of an object; you can imagine it as the amount of wrapping paper needed to cover it exactly. For square and rectangular shapes, the surface area consists of the sum of the areas of the faces. This is particularly easy with a cube because each face has the same area and there are six faces; the surface area of a cube of edge s is $6s^2$. For the less obviously measured shapes, try to separate the surfaces into discreet pieces. For instance, in a cylinder the surface area is the sum of the areas of the top and bottom circles—πr^2 times 2—added to the area of the tubular section (sort of like where the label on a can of soup would go). To see how we find the area of that section, first imagine drawing a slit down its side.

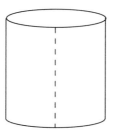

(It's a bit like peeling that soup label off of the can.) You end up with a rectangle, which is also called a cylinder's **lateral area**.

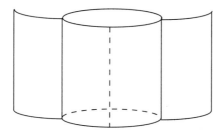

Lateral area is the area of a shape's surface, excluding its top and base. To get the area of the rectangle, multiply the base times the height. And what is the length of the base? Why, the circumference of the circle, of course.

To find the surface area of a cone, you need the area of the circle that is its base, and then the lateral area of the cone itself. The formula for this lateral area is rs, in which s is the **slant height** of the cone, measured from the vertex to an edge of the base circle.

The surface area of a sphere is $4\pi r^2$.

Example

What are the surface area and volume of the right cylinder pictured?

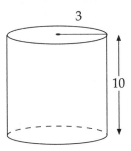

We'll start with the surface area simply because that's mentioned first. The area of the top and bottom circles of the cylinder are part of the overall surface area. The radius of these circles, which are equal, is 3. So the area of each circle is 9π (from $A = \pi r^2$). Since there are two of them, their combined area is 18π. Now for the cylinder's lateral area: We know from the diagram that the height is 10; the length is the circumference of the circles that form the base and top. Since the radius of the circle is 3, the circumference is 6π (from $c = 2\pi r$). So the area of the rectangle is 6π times 10, or 60π. Add this to the area of the circles, which is 18π, and the entire surface area of the figure is 78π.

As for the volume, it's simply the area of one dimension—the circle—times the additional dimension. In this case the height of the figure is handy. The area of the circle is 9π and the height of the cylinder is 10, so the volume is 90π.

EXERCISE 9.1

Drawing the figures for these questions yourself will probably help you more than we can ever adequately describe.

1. What is the volume of a cylinder with a height of 5 and a base with a radius of 3? What is its surface area?

2. What is the radius of a sphere whose volume is 36π? What is its surface area?

3. What is the volume of a rectangular prism with dimensions of 3, 5, and 7? What is its surface area?

4. What is the volume of a cylinder whose height is twice its base radius, r?

5. A cylinder with a base radius of 2 and a height of 3 is inscribed in a sphere. What is the surface area of the sphere?

6. A cube is inscribed in a sphere of radius r. What is the ratio of their volumes?

7. A cone with a height of h is cut by a plane parallel to its base that divides it into two shapes of equal volume. At what distance from the top of the cone does this plane cut?

8. A sphere is inscribed in a cylinder with a base radius of r whose height is the diameter of the sphere. What is the ratio of the volume of the cylinder to the volume of the sphere?

ANSWERS TO CHAPTER NINE EXERCISES

ANSWERS TO EXERCISE 9.1

1. Volume = 45π; surface area = 48π

2. Radius = 3; surface area = 36π

3. Volume = 105; surface area = 142

4. $2\pi r^3$

5. 25π

   A line can be drawn, dividing the cylinder from one edge to the opposite, so a cross-section of the middle forms a right triangle, which has (Pythagorean Theorem) a hypotenuse of 5, which would also be a diameter of the sphere.

6. $\dfrac{2\sqrt{3}}{3\pi}$

   The diagonal of the sphere forms a triangle within the cube in which its side is one leg, its diagonal across the bottom is the other (the side of the cube times the square root of two because of the ratio of an isosceles right triangle), and the diagonal of the sphere is the hypotenuse. Using the Pythagorean Theorem, solve for the side of the cube in terms of r. Then rationalize the fraction and you're home free.

7. $\dfrac{h}{\sqrt[3]{2}}$

This one is tricky. You set up the problem algebraically, realizing that the radius and the height will be lessened by the same degree. Be careful though, when setting this up, to note that this means the unknown that divides the radius will be squared, like so:

$$\frac{1}{2}\left(\frac{1}{3}\pi r^2 h\right) = \frac{1}{3}\,\pi\,\frac{r^2}{x^2}\,\frac{h}{x}$$

This will give you the place at which h is cut; it won't be cut just in the middle, of course, because a cone tapers as it goes up, and this wouldn't give you equal volumes.

8. $\dfrac{3}{2}$

Since the radius of the cylinder is also the radius of the sphere (remember, the sphere is inscribed), and the height of the cylinder is the diameter, this means that the height is twice the radius. So the volume of the cylinder is $\pi r^2 \cdot 2r$, and the volume of the sphere is $\dfrac{4}{3}\pi r^3$. Put the volume of the cylinder over the volume of the sphere, and simplify.

10

Analytic Geometry

Now that you know the basic components of geometric shapes and forms, it's time to see the happy place where geometry and algebra meet. The site of this wonderful meeting is the **coordinate plane**, also known as the **Cartesian grid**; it looks like this.

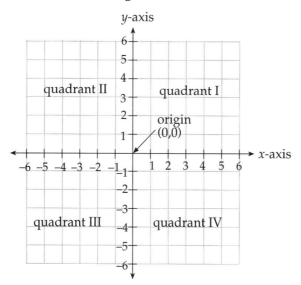

The two lines making up the center of the grid are the **axes** (pronounced acks-eeze); the **y-axis** is vertical, and the **x-axis** is horizontal. The place where the two axes meet is at the 0 point on both of them; this point is called the **origin** of the graph or grid. As you can see, the axes split the space into four spaces; these spaces are called **quadrants**. The quadrants are numbered in counter-clockwise fashion, starting with the upper right: Quadrants I, II, III and IV. Grids like this are used to plot points that make up lines and shapes. It's the coordinate *plane*, after all, and planes are made up of an infinity of points. A point is also called a **coordinate pair**, because each point is identified by two coordinates, an **x-coordinate** and a **y-coordinate**. The first coordinate of a pair is the x-coordinate and the second is the y-coordinate. An example might be (3, 5). The x-coordinate of this point is 3, and the y-coordinate is 5. To locate this point on the graph, simply count over three on the x-axis— you'll move to the right to get to the positive 3—and up five on the y-axis. The point you reach is (3, 5) in quadrant I.

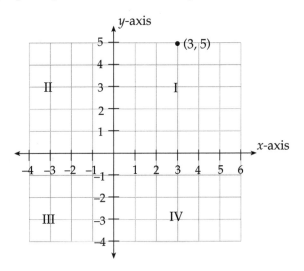

All points with two positive coordinates will be located in quadrant I. Look at the numbers on the axes to get a clear picture of this; you can also see that points in quadrant II have a negative x-coordinate and a positive y-coordinate. Points in quadrant III have two negative coordinates, and points in quadrant IV have a positive x-coordinate and a negative y-coordinate.

EXERCISE 10.1

For the following questions, plot the points given on the graph below, and label them by their letters.

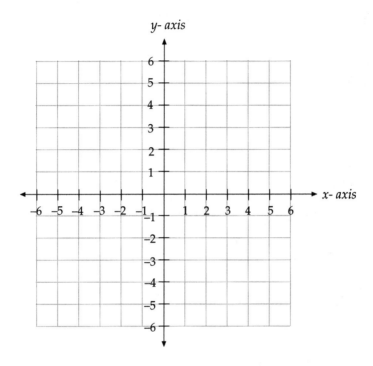

1. *a* (5, 3)

2. *b* (0, 1)

3. *c* (–1, 3)

4. *d* (2, –2)

5. *e* (–3, 0)

6. *f* (–1, –1)

7. *g* (1, –5)

8. *h* (–5, –1)

LINES

What happens when points are joined? They form lines, and the first kinds of lines that we are going to address are straight lines.

LINEAR EQUATIONS REDUX:
STRAIGHT LINES AND THEIR PROPERTIES

Equations are expressed in lots of different ways. Now is the time to express them graphically. The expression of an equation is called a **graph** or **locus**. Of course, the space they're drawn on is also sometimes called a graph. Not to worry, the context of a question will almost always show you which type of graph is referred to. The first type of equation we will attempt (and conquer, no doubt) is the linear equation. You've seen linear equations before (page 15 if they don't ring a bell), and probably, possibly, you didn't wonder too much about why they were called linear equations. The mystery is now solved: They are called linear equations because they are equations that form lines. Let's look at an example: $y = 3x + 2$

To express this equation graphically, substitute in values for x or y; substituting for x is probably easier. Thus, if x is 0, y is 2, and you have a coordinate pair, (0, 2). If x is 1, y is 5, yielding another coordinate pair, (1, 5). To create the line, plot these two points on the graph.

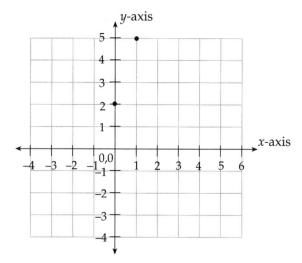

Once you have two points you have a line; simply draw through the two points. Voila. The graph of a linear equation.

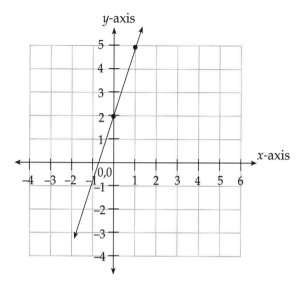

Every (x, y) pair that works in that equation $y = 3x + 2$ exists somewhere on this line.

SIMULTANEOUS EQUATIONS, ONE MORE TIME

What were you finding, really, when you found the values of x and y for a linear equation system back on page 15? You were finding the point of intersection of two *different* lines. That's what the values of x and y that worked for both linear equations were, they were the coordinates of the point at which the lines intersect. And lines are exactly what those equations were depicting.

SLOPE

Have you ever tried to go up a hill on a bicycle, or in a car, or on your own tired feet? If you have, you've probably noticed that you can get pretty exhausted if the hill is steep. You're a lot happier when you approach a hill that isn't as steep, right? Well, that dread or relief on approaching a hill is an expression of your mathematical astuteness, because when you notice the steepness of a hill, you're noticing its **slope**. Slope is the measure of the steepness of a line; mathematically it's represented by the letter m. To calculate the slope of a line, put the difference between two y-coordinates over the difference between two corresponding x-coordinates:

$$m = \frac{y_2 - y_1}{x_2 - x_1}$$

The slope of the line we just graphed, $y = 3x + 2$, can be calculated by the coordinates we identified, (0, 2) and (1, 5). The expression of these coordinate pairs in the formula for slope is $\frac{5-2}{1-0}$, or 3. Thus, the slope of the line is 3.

There is a sneaky little shortcut for finding the slope of certain lines, though. The linear equation we've been working with here is $y = 3x + 2$ which is in the form $y = mx + b$. What is m again? Why, it's the slope. So, if you ever see a linear equation in this particular form, the slope (m) is the coefficient of x. And many times, if the equation isn't already in this form you can put it in this form.

Example

What is the slope of the line that is represented by the equation $y + 5 = x$?

There are two ways to find the slope here: you could use the slope formula, or you could put the equation into the form $y = mx + b$. We'll try the second, easier way first, and then go through the formula for good measure.

To put the equation into $y = mx + b$ form, what must you do? Well, clearly the y needs to be isolated.

Subtract 5 from both sides.

$$y + 5 - 5 = x - 5$$

This gives you $y = x - 5$. You now have the equation in $y = mx + b$ form. The coefficient for x is 1, so the slope of the line is 1.

How do we go about putting this equation into the slope formula? Well, the formula needs two coordinate pairs. The line's equation is $y + 5 = x$; if $y = 0$ then $x = 5$, and if $y = 1$ then $x = 6$. The slope formula is the difference in y-coordinates over the difference in x-coordinates. You get $\frac{1-0}{6-5}$, also known as 1. Pretty slick, no?

SLIPPERY SLOPES

When is a hill not a hill? When it's flat. A flat, or horizontal, line is a line whose y-coordinate is constant. All horizontal lines have the same slope: 0. That's because there is no change in y, so you have a fraction with the numerator 0, which is always equal to 0.

Vertical lines, on the other hand, have an x-coordinate which is constant. This means that they form fractions with 0 denominators, that are undefined; this means that *the slope of a vertical line is undefined*.

A positive slope indicates a line that rises to the right, and a negative slope indicates a line that falls to the right.

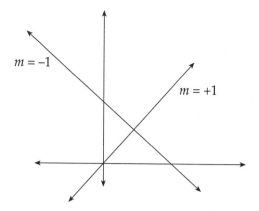

The numerical value of the slope—which is the absolute value if the slope is negative—represents the steepness of a slope and the angle that the slope makes with the x-axis. Thus, a line of slope $\frac{1}{2}$ is less steep than a line of slope 1, which in turn is less steep than a line of slope 2.

Parallel lines must have equal slopes, which makes sense if you think about it. So if you come across two distinct lines with the same slope, they must be parallel. Perpendicular lines, on the other hand, must have slopes that multiply together to equal −1. Do you see now how geometry and algebra meet? If you see two algebraic lines— linear equations—$y = 2x + 3$ and $y = -\frac{1}{2}x + 2$, you now know a geometric fact about them: They're perpendicular, because $\left(-\frac{1}{2}\right)(2) = -1$.

WHAT THE HECK IS THE *b*?

In the equation $y = mx + b$, you know that the m is the slope, and the x and y are the x- and y-coordinates. So what the heck is the b? The b is the **y-intercept**. The y-intercept is the point on a line at which it intercepts the y-axis, which is the point at which the x-coordinate equals 0. There is also an **x-intercept**; it's the point at which the line intercepts the x-axis; at which the y-coordinate equals 0. The way to find the y-coordinate if the equation isn't in the form $y = mx + b$ is to substitute $x = 0$ into the equation; this will give you the point at which the line intercepts the y-axis. To find the x-intercept, substitute in $y = 0$.

Example

What is the x-intercept of the line $3x - y = 2$?

Well, we could put the equation into the form $y = mx + b$, but that won't help us find the x-intercept, because b represents the y-intercept. How do we find the x-intercept? We substitute in $y = 0$. We get $3x = 2$, so $x = \frac{2}{3}$. The line intercepts the x-axis at the point at which x equals $\frac{2}{3}$.

DISTANCE

Let's say you have two points on your grid, (2, 3) and (6, 3).

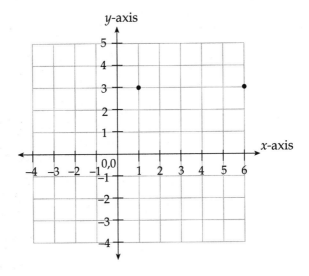

To calculate the distance between them is a fairly easy matter; just count along the x-axis, or subtract the x-coordinates, and you've found the distance between the points. What if, however, the two points did not exist along such an easily countable stretch? Take a look at these points, for instance.

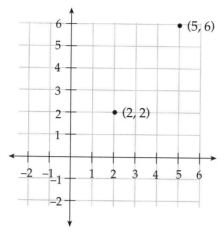

The distance between them does not appear to be so easily measured. However, there is a formula that's designed to determine the distance between two points. There seems to be a formula for everything, doesn't there? Before we get to this specific formula though, let's take a moment to see how it works.

Whenever you have two points on a graph that are not horizontally or vertically aligned, you also have the makings of a right triangle; the line between the two points forms the hypotenuse. You can see it with the two points on the grid below.

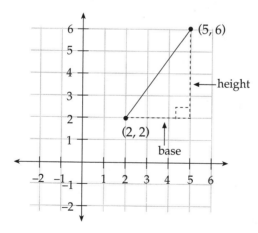

The length of this triangle's legs can be counted out: The height is 4 and the base is 3. To find the length of the hypotenuse we fall back on that reliable old friend the Pythagorean Theorem: $a^2 + b^2 = c^2$. Thus, in this case $4^2 + 3^2 = c^2$, or $16 + 9 = c^2$, or $25 = c^2$, and $c = 5$. The distance between your two selected points is 5. The **distance formula** simply makes this process more regular; it says that $\sqrt{(x_2 - x_1)^2 + (y_2 - y_1)^2}$

represents the distance between two points, x_1, y_1 and x_2, y_2. As you can see, it's exactly how we treated the points above, but by giving it an algebraic formula we can fix it as a more useful truth.

HALFWAY THERE

There's one more formula that relates to lines and their equations, and you might want to have it on hand in case anyone ever asks you, "Hey, would you happen to know the midpoint of the line between two points, (x_1, y_1) and (x_2, y_2)?"

Okay, so that might not happen. But on the theory that it's always best to be prepared (and the hunch that you're going to face a question like this on a test somewhere), here it is. The midpoint of a line between two points (x_1, y_1) and (x_2, y_2) has coordinates

$$x = \frac{x_1 + x_2}{2}, \text{ and } y = \frac{y_1 + y_2}{2}$$

Seems pretty obvious, doesn't it? Well it is. Go ahead and enjoy it, you deserve an easy and obvious formula by now.

EXERCISE 10.2

1. What is the slope of a line that includes the points (3, 2) and (2, 1)?

2. What is the distance between the points mentioned above? What is their midpoint?

3. What is the y-intercept of the line defined above?

4. What is the equation for the line defined above?

5. Is the line $2y - 10 = 2x$ parallel to the line defined above?

6. What is the equation for a line through $(-3, 4)$ which is perpendicular to the line defined in questions 1 through 4?

7. What is the distance between $(-3, 4)$ and the y-intercept of the line $3y - 2 = 3x$?

8. What is the y-intercept of the line through $(-3, 4)$ and perpendicular to $2y - 10 = 2x$?

FUNCTIONS

That's all very well and good, you may be thinking, but what was all that hooey about this being the place where algebra and geometry meet? And what's the use of a graph? Here's the short answer: Graphs and coordinates can be used to express and solve algebra problems; graphs serve as a link between the two heretofore separate worlds of algebra and geometry. Linking these two gives you, the eager student, a more complete understanding of mathematics at the same time that it allows you to move further into mathematics. Now that you can recognize certain equations as representing straight lines, it's time for you to recognize another subset of equations: **functions**.

A function is an expression of one variable's dependency on another. Remember back to when you were learning to write formulas. You were expressing interrelationships among variables. For instance, *the retail price of an item is three times its wholesale price* could be expressed as $r = 3w$. The retail price is a function of the wholesale price. The circumference of a circle is a function of its diameter, as $c = \pi d$. The price of a magazine subscription is 67 percent of its newsstand price, $s = 67\% n$, and s is a function of n. All of these can correspond to the statement y is a function of x, which is expressed mathematically as $y = f(x)$. This expression does not mean that f is a quantity or that there is any multiplication going on, it only indicates that the variable y is a function of the variable x. More specifically, the value of y depends on the value of x, thus y is called the **dependent variable** and x is called the **independent variable**. This means that the value of x is assigned without reference to the value of y, and the value of y is a result of this value of x. For each possible value of x, a function presents *only one* possible value of y. That's important enough to put in a box.

> For each possible value of x, a function presents *only one* possible value of y.

Perhaps you are already seeing how functions coincide with coordinate planes. It turns out that the most common way of expressing a function is graphically, with each point of the function plotted and joined to form some kind of line. These particular graphs are the graphs of functions.

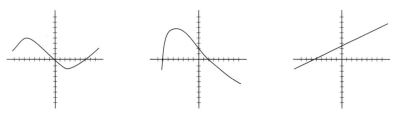

One great way to tell whether a graphed shape or line is a function is to imagine scanning it with a vertical line. If the graph has two points of intersection on a vertical line, it's not a function.

This is called the **vertical line test**, and it shows that you can get a lot of information from a graph itself.

HOW TO SKETCH A GRAPH

The basic way to sketch the graph of an equation, whether it's a function or anything else, is to enter values for the possible coordinates, just as you would with the equation for an ordinary line. For function equations, since the y is dependent, it's easiest to enter values for x and then find the value of y that results. Thus, for the function $f(x) = 3x^3 + 2$, if x is 0, y is 2, and the first plotted point is (0, 2). Enter other values for x, such as x is –1, which means that $y = -1$; then x is 1, which means that $y = 5$; and x is –2, which sends y down and off of the part of our coordinate plane that is visible.

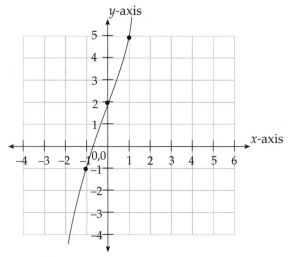

Then draw a line connecting the dots—see, it's almost like a game—in the line or curve that seems appropriate. The more points there are, the easier it is to see the exact shape, but as you become familiar with the shapes that show up over and over, you'll see that usually, even having a few points is enough.

We can express the graph of the function $r = 3w$ (discussed above) on the coordinate plane as a function of x where $y = f(x) = 3x$.

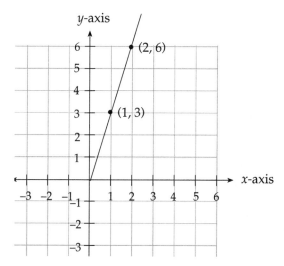

We usually use x and y in order to lend some consistency, though functions can use any letters they care to for variables. For instance, the function itself could be expressed as $r = g(w) = 3w$ or $y = t(x) = 3x$ or just $f(x) = 3x$; if the question makes it clear that you're dealing with a function, it doesn't matter what particular variables are used. The more important issue is being able to tell which of the variables is the dependent variable and which is independent.

The set of possible values for x of a particular function is called the **domain** of the function, and the set of all possible values for x as well as the corresponding values for y is called the **range** of a function.

EVALUATING FUNCTIONS

Functions are sometimes expressed with numbers already in them, like so: $f(4)$ in which $f(x) = x^3 + 2$. This is asking you to calculate the function for the number 4; simply put the number 4 into the formula and evaluate. You get $4^3 + 2$, which is 66. So $f(4)$ is 66. Evaluating functions is easy as long as you follow the directions given and take your time. Try a few on your own.

EXERCISE 10.3

1. If $f(x) = 2x - 1$, find $f(0)$, $f(1)$, and $f(2)$.

2. Express the area of a circle as a function of its radius.

3. If $f(x) = 3x^3 + 2x - 1$, find $f(1)$ and $f(2)$.

4. Express the perimeter of a square as a function of its side s.

5. If $g(e) = 3e - 2$, what is $g(3)$?

6. Express the time taken to travel a distance of 60 miles as a function of rate.

7. If $f(d) = d^3 - 2d - 1$, what is $f(f(d))$?

8. Express the distance traveled at a rate of 50 miles per hour as a function of time.

CIRCLES

One graph that is clearly not a function is the graph that represents the circle. Just try putting the circle through the vertical line test. Circles can still be graphed, however, and the first thing we'll do is show you how to recognize their equations. Let's take a look at a circle in a coordinate plane.

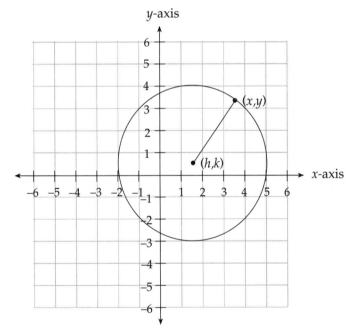

For a circle with a center at (h, k) and a radius r, and any point on the circle (x, y), the equation for the circle is $(x - h)^2 + (y - k)^2 = r^2$. Notice any resemblance to the distance formula?

You can obtain an awful lot of information about a circle by looking at its equation. If you are presented with the equation $(x - 4)^2 + (y - 2)^2 = 16$, you know that you are dealing with a circle of radius 4—the square root of 16—whose center is at (4, 2).

A circle whose center is at the origin is represented by the equation $x^2 + y^2 = r^2$, because here h and k are both equal to 0.

MANIPULATING CIRCLE EQUATIONS

A circle's equation is sometimes presented in a slightly different form, for instance, $x^2 - 8x + y^2 - 4y + 4 = 0$. You already have the means to deal with an irritating mess like this, you may remember it from page 62—completing the square. To complete the square in this situation, proceed as you would normally, by moving the numerical term to the other side of the equation, and then putting in the third term of each equation, which is half of the coefficient of the middle term, squared.

Here we go:

$x^2 - 8x + y^2 - 4y + 4 = 0$ becomes $(x^2 - 8x + \quad) + (y^2 - 4y + \quad) = -4$

Complete the square.

$$(x^2 - 8x + 16) + (y^2 - 4y + 4) = -4 + 16 + 4$$
$$(x - 4)^2 + (y - 2)^2 = 16$$

Does this form of the equation look familiar? Of course it does; it's the equation for a circle that you were introduced to a few short paragraphs ago. This circle has a center at (4, 2) and a radius of 4.

FREAKY CIRCLE STUFF

What would happen if you came up with an equation set equal to 0? For instance, $(x - 3)^2 + (y - 2)^2 = 0$? Since this essentially expresses a circle of radius 0, what this equation represents is a point; the point in this case is (−3, −2). You will sometimes hear an equation such as this referred to as a **point circle**.

If an equation yields a negative radius, for instance, if the equation is something like $(x + 5)^2 + (y - 1)^2 = -25$, the circle is imaginary.

Example

What is the equation of a circle with center (2, −3) that passes through point (5, 1)?

Here you have the (x, y) point of the equation: (5, 1), plus the center, h, k: (2, −3). You can set up your equation then, $(5 - 2)^2 + (1 - (-3))^2 = r^2$. You get $9 + 16 = r^2$, or $25 = r^2$, or $r = 5$. Thus the equation for the circle is $(x - 2)^2 + (y + 3)^2 = 25$.

INTERCEPTIONS

Circles, depending on where their centers are, sometimes intercept the x-axis, the y-axis, or both. They can touch an axis in one place, which means that the circle is **tangent** to the axis, or intercept the axis in two places. How do you determine where these places are? You find these intercepts in much the same way you find them for linear equations. To find out where a circle intercepts the x-axis, set y equal to 0 in the circle equation and solve for x. If there is only one possible value for x, the circle is tangent. If there are two, it intercepts the x-axis twice; if x is imaginary (a negative square root, remember?), the circle doesn't intercept the x-axis.

This works to determine if and where circles intercept particular lines as well as the axes. In the case of a particular line, for instance, $x = 2$, substitute 2 in for x in the equation and solve the equation for y.

Example

At what point does the circle $(x - 4)^2 + (y - 2)^2 = 16$ intercept the x-axis? Where does it intercept the y-axis?

To find out where the circle intercepts the x-axis, set y equal to 0.

$$(x - 4)^2 + (0 - 2)^2 = 16$$
$$(x - 4)^2 + 4 = 16$$
$$(x - 4)^2 = 12$$
$$x - 4 = \pm\sqrt{12}$$

There are two solutions:

$$x - 4 = +\sqrt{12}$$
$$x - 4 = +2\sqrt{3}$$
$$x = 2\sqrt{3} + 4$$

The other solution:

$$x - 4 = -\sqrt{12}$$
$$x = -\sqrt{12} + 4$$
$$x = -2\sqrt{3} + 4$$

These are the two points where the circle intercepts the x-axis. To find where the circle intercepts the y-axis, set x equal to 0.

$$(0 - 4)^2 + (y - 2)^2 = 16$$
$$16 + (y - 2)^2 = 16$$
$$(y - 2)^2 = 0$$
$$y = 2$$

Since there's only one possible value for y, the circle is tangent to the y-axis at the point $(0, 2)$. Notice also that this is because the radius is equal to the distance from the center to the origin along the x-axis.

EXERCISE 10.4

1. What is the radius of a circle with equation $x^2 + y^2 - 4x + 2y - 20 = 0$?

2. What is the center of the circle above?

3. Where does the line $y = 4$ intersect the circle above?

4. What is the equation for a circle in the coordinate system with center $(2, 5)$ and radius 3?

5. What is the radius and center of a circle with equation $x^2 + (y - 2)^2 = 9$?

6. At what points does the circle above intercept the y-axis?

7. What is the radius and center of a circle with the equation $x^2 + y^2 = 0$?

8. At what point does the circle with the equation $x^2 + y^2 - 16x - 16y - 41 = 0$ touch the x-axis?

ANSWERS TO CHAPTER TEN EXERCISES

ANSWERS TO EXERCISE 10.1

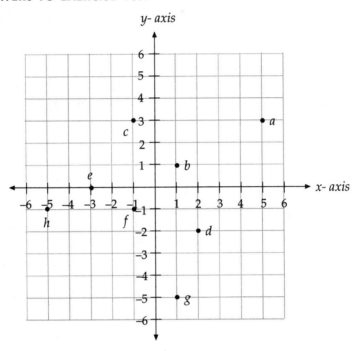

ANSWERS TO EXERCISE 10.2

1. The slope is 1.

2. $\sqrt{2}$

3. -1
   (Use one of the points, (3, 2) for example, in an equation of the $y = mx + b$ format; you already know that $m = 1$, so solve for b.)

4. $y = x - 1$

5. Yes
   Put the new line into the $y = mx + b$ formula and note that it has a slope of 1 as well, but is a distinct line from the first line. Thus, it's parallel.

6. $y = -x + 1$
   The same equation but a different slope.

7. $\sqrt{\dfrac{91}{9}}$ or $\dfrac{\sqrt{91}}{3}$

8. 1

You know that m must be –1 in order to be perpendicular to the first line, so use $y = mx + b$ with the point given, and solve for b.

ANSWERS TO EXERCISE 10.3

1. $f(0) = -1$, $f(1) = 1$, $f(2) = 3$

2. $f(r)$ or $A = \pi r^2$

3. $f(1) = 4$, $f(2) = 27$

4. $f(s)$ or $P = 4s$

5. $g(3) = 7$

6. $f(r)$ or $T = \dfrac{60}{R}$

7. $f(f(d)) = (d^3 - 2d - 1)^3 - 2(d^3 - 2d - 1) - 1$, which becomes $d^9 - 10d^3 + 4d$

8. $f(T)$ or $D = 50T$

ANSWERS TO EXERCISE 10.4

1. radius = 5

2. the center = (2, –1)

3. at point (2, 4)
   This is the only point on the circle that exists this high up, based on the radius and the center. To find this point, substitute $y = 4$ into the equation for the circle and find the corresponding x coordinate.

4. $(x - 2)^2 + (y - 5)^2 = 9$

5. radius 3, center (0, 2)

6. $y = 5, -1$

7. center (0, 0), no radius—it's a point circle

8. It intercepts the x-axis at $x = 5$ and $x = -21$.

Parabolas

CURVED LINES

As you have seen (and will see, again and again), equations can be expressed graphically. So far you've graphed straight lines and circles. There are (surprise, surprise) other kinds of shapes and lines that correspond to other types of equations. You can now recognize a linear equation as the equation for a straight line, and you can also recognize equations for circles. But what about the other equations you've been working with in your algebra chapters—what about quadratic equations? What types of shapes do they correspond to?

How lucky it is that you happen to wonder this! The graph of a quadratic equation presents a special type of shape to be graphed: The **parabola**. A parabola is a particular type of curved line. There are certain curved lines called conic sections, or conics, that have the following wonderful property: All of their points maintain equal ratios from a fixed point or points called the focus or foci, and (sometimes) a fixed external line called the **directrix**. A parabola is a type of conic section whose points maintain a one-to-one ratio from the focus and the directrix.

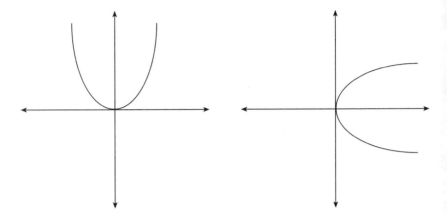

Here are the diagrams that show how each point on the curve maintains a 1:1 ratio of distance between it and the focus, and it and the directrix. On the following diagrams, $\frac{c}{c} = \frac{d}{d}$.

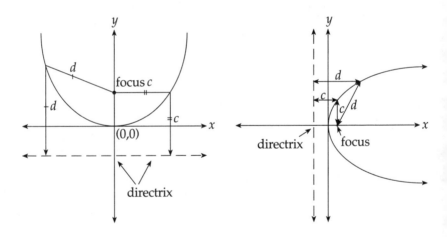

PARABOLA EQUATIONS

To explain how the equation for a parabola is derived we will look at the simplest parabola, one that opens upward and whose vertex is at the origin.

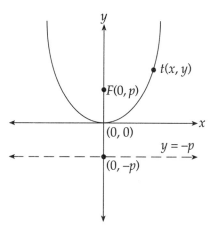

The focus, which we'll call F, is at $(0, p)$ and the directrix, which we'll call D, is the line with the equation $y = -p$. Every point on this parabola is equally distant from the focus, $(0, p)$ and from the directrix, $y = -p$. Any point on the parabola will be known as t, with coordinates (x, y)—old friends of yours. Now, to produce an equation for this parabola, we're going to go a few pages back, to something you just learned (or were reminded of)—the distance formula. As you may remember, the distance formula is $\sqrt{(x_2 - x_1) + (y_2 - y_1)^2}$. Take a look at the diagram to orient yourself. The formula for a parabola rests on the fact that all the points are equally distant from the focus and the directrix. We will use tF to express the distance between the focus and point t, and tD to express the distance between the directrix and point t. Thus an equation of their distances is: $tF = tD$. To express this in terms of its particular coordinates we can use the distance formula to calculate those distances, tF and tD. The equation for tF—the distance from (x, y) to $(0, p)$—is this: $\sqrt{(x - 0)^2 + (y - p)^2}$. And the equation for tD—the distance from (x, y) to $y = -p$—is this: $\sqrt{(x - x)^2 + (y - (-p))^2}$. So, $tF = tD$ is expressed like this:

$$\sqrt{(x - 0)^2 + (y - p)^2} = \sqrt{(x - x)^2 + (y - (-p))^2}$$

Look at the diagram to see where the coordinates are, so that you can visualize these distances.

Next, you can simplify this so that the whole equation looks like this: $\sqrt{x^2 + (y-p)^2} = y + p$. To simplify further, square both sides to form

$$x^2 + y^2 - {}^2py + p^2 = y^2 + 2py + p^2$$

Can the equation be simplified further? You're an old hand at this, of course it can.

$$x^2 + y^2 - 2py + p^2 = y^2 + 2py + p^2$$

$$x^2 - 2py = 2py$$

$$x^2 = 4py$$

You can also present it in terms of y, if you like. You get $y = \dfrac{x^2}{4p}$.

This $y = \dfrac{x^2}{4p}$ is the formula for a parabola of the type you see here, right-side up with its vertex at the origin. Vertex, you say? The vertex is the point on the parabola that is intersected by a line drawn through the focus and perpendicular to the directrix. A parabola that opened down would have its vertex at its topmost point; this parabola has its vertex at its bottom-most point. The line that intersects the parabola at the vertex, by the way, and goes through the focus perpendicular to the directrix is called the axis of the parabola.

Is a right-side up parabola a function? Sure it is—try the vertical line test.

UPSIDE-DOWN?!?

There are parabolas that open down, like so:

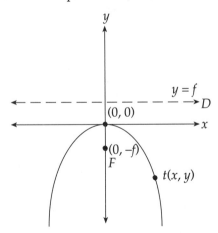

with the directrix above the focus. In this case, the formula for the parabola is $x^2 = -4py$, in which p is a positive number representing, as shown, the distance from the vertex of the parabola to the focus.

ALL AROUND THE TOWN

What about the parabola that opens to the side? Perhaps you can guess the difference in how it is expressed. The equation for a parabola that opens to the side is derived in the same way, but it is along the x-axis and its equation is $y^2 = 4px$, which is also known as $x = \dfrac{y^2}{4p}$. These represent parabolas that open to the right; parabolas that open to the left are expressed by $y^2 = -4px$, which is the same as $x = \dfrac{y^2}{4p}$. Are these parabolas functions? No, because they have more than one value of y for each value of x.

$x^2 = 4py$ or $y = \dfrac{x^2}{4p}$ represents

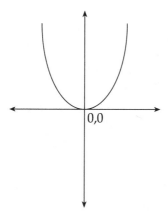

$x^2 = -4py$ or $-\dfrac{x^2}{4p}$ represents

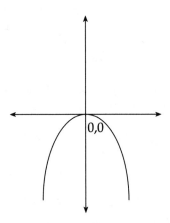

$y^2 = 4px$ or $x = \dfrac{y^2}{4p}$ represents

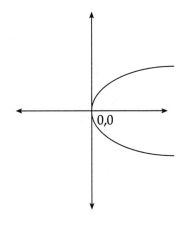

$y^2 = -4px$ or $x = -\dfrac{y^2}{4p}$ represents

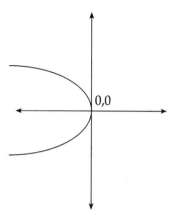

Notice that these all represent parabolas whose vertices are at the origin of the (x, y) coordinate system. Take a look at an example that deals with a parabola of this type.

Example

What are the focus and directrix of the parabola $x^2 = 2y$?

To answer a question like this, study the information presented in the equation. From the positive coefficient of y, as well as the fact that the x is raised to the second power (you will soon have memorized this information), we see that it's a parabola that opens up. Since $x^2 = 4py$ is how you know the standard parabola equation, the $2y$ of our equation represents the $4py$. That means $4p = 2$, so $p = \dfrac{1}{2}$. Since the parabola's vertex is at the origin, its focus must have an x-coordinate of 0. If p is $\dfrac{1}{2}$, the focus is $(0, \dfrac{1}{2})$. Can you see where its directrix might be? Since every point on a parabola must be equally distant from its focus and its directrix, and the focus in this case is $\dfrac{1}{2}$ from the origin, then the directrix must also be $\dfrac{1}{2}$ from the origin, but in the other direction. Thus, the directrix is the line $y = -\dfrac{1}{2}$.

EXERCISE 11.1

1. What is the focus of the parabola $x^2 = 8y$? What is the equation of the directrix? In what direction does it open? Is it a function?

2. What is the focus of the parabola $\dfrac{y^2}{4} = x$? What is the equation of the directrix? In what direction does it open? Is it a function?

3. What is the focus of the parabola $x^2 = -y$? What is the equation of the directrix? In what direction does it open? Is it a function?

4. What is the equation of a parabola with its vertex at the origin and a focus of $(0, 5)$? What is the equation of its directrix? Is it a function?

5. What is the focus of the parabola $4y^2 = -5x$? What is the equation of the directrix? In what direction does it open? Is it a function?

6. What is the equation of a parabola with its vertex at the origin and a focus of $(0, 2)$? What is the equation of its directrix? Is it a function?

7. What is the focus of the parabola $-x^2 = -8y$? What is the equation of the directrix? In what direction does it open? Is it a function?

8. What is the focus of the parabola $y^2 = \dfrac{4x}{2}$? What is the equation of the directrix? In what direction does it open? Is it a function?

PARABOLAS WITH VERTICES ELSEWHERE

Wouldn't life be wonderful if all parabolas had their vertices resting softly on the origin? Sadly, as we all know by now, life is more complicated and less agreeable than that. Parabolas can have vertices all over the coordinate system, in any quadrant they feel like settling in. What are the equations for parabolas of this type? You may recognize them as your somewhat long-lost friends: $y = ax^2 + bx + c$, in which $a \neq 0$, and $x = ay^2 + by + c$ in which $a \neq 0$. Another way you will see these equations expressed is $4p(y - k) = (x - h)^2$. These forms are the same equations expressed differently, with different variables. Read on to learn how to go from one equation to the other, and what the variables in the equations tell you.

How do these work? Let's look at an example in which $y = ax^2 + bx + c$.

Example

How about $y = x^2 - 8x + 21$?

First of all, you should know that when a is a positive number (remember that a is the coefficient of the squared term) the parabola opens upwards. Beyond that, in order to show how this expression is related to the now familiar $x^2 = 4py$, we need to do some rearrangement.

The way we will rearrange the equation is to set it up so that we can complete the square of the squared term, in this case, x. The first step to completing the square is to move the 21.

$$y - 21 = x^2 - 8x + 21 - 21$$
$$y - 21 = x^2 - 8x$$

Now, complete the square by taking half of the coefficient of x, squaring it, and adding it to both sides.

$$y - 21 + 16 = x^2 - 8x + 16$$

Now, factor.

$$y - 5 = (x - 4)^2$$

How is this related to $4py = x^2$? Well, look at these expressions as whole terms. For instance, $x - 4$ is the term being squared here, just like x, and $y - 5$ is the term being multiplied by $4p$ (in this case it's clearly equal to 1, which explains its invisibility).

Rearranging the equation in this way, and noticing what it has in common with a parabola whose vertex is on the origin, is extremely useful. The equation has been transformed from $ax^2 + bx + c$ into $4p(y - k) = (x - h)^2$. Why is this form so useful? Because in $4p(y - k) = (x - h)^2$, the h and the k represent the coordinates of the vertex of the parabola. That means that this particular parabola, $y - 5 = (x - 4)^2$, has its vertex at the point (4, 5). It's as though the equation is setting up its own set of axes on the coordinate system, and the point of origin is at the point (h, k). Putting the equation into the $4p(y - k) = (x - h)^2$ form allows you to access these values more easily.

Take a look at your general equation again, $4p(y - k) = (x - h)^2$. If you wanted the graph of a parabola whose vertex was on the origin, that would mean its vertex was at (0, 0) and h, k were both 0; your equation would be this: $4p(y - 0) = (x - 0)^2$, exactly what we have already described as the equation for a parabola whose vertex is at the origin, $4py = x^2$.

What are the focus and directrix of the parabola $y - 5 = (x - 4)^2$? Well, the focus is still a distance of p away from the vertex. In this case, since your equation is $y - 5 = (x - 4)^2$ the vertex is at $(4, 5)$. And what is p, you ask? Well, the equation for a parabola is $4p(y - k) = (x - h)^2$. Thus, $(y - 5)$ has a coefficient of 1, which represents the $4p$. If $4p$ is 1, then $p = \frac{1}{4}$. The focus is thus $\frac{1}{4}$ above 5 (our y-coordinate for the vertex). The focus is $(4, 5\frac{1}{4})$. And the directrix? Well, the directrix is the distance p below the vertex, $(4, 5)$, at the line $y = 4\frac{3}{4}$.

How did we know that the focus was above the vertex and the directrix was below it? Because the coefficient of y was positive, meaning that the parabola opened upwards.

Some parabolas look wider, some look narrower. If they all have to have the same general curve, how can they look so different? Here's how to look at it: The more broadly curved parabolas are essentially the same narrower-looking parabolas with the curved vertices magnified.

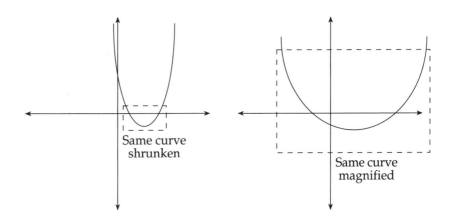

Same curve shrunken

Same curve magnified

GENERAL EQUATIONS FOR PARABOLAS

$y = ax^2 + bx + c$ and $(x - h)^2 = 4p(y - k)$ open upwards.

$y = -ax^2 + bx + c$ and $(x - h)^2 = -4p(y - k)$ open downwards.

$x = ay^2 + by + c$ and $(y - k)^2 = 4p(x - h)$ open toward the positive side of the x-axis.

$x = -ay^2 + by + c$ and $(y - k)^2 = -4p(x - h)$ open toward the negative side of the x-axis.

Example

If $4y = 4x^2 + 16x - 24$, what direction does the graphed parabola open toward, what is its focus, what is its vertex, and what is its directrix? Is it a function?

To answer this series of questions, we need to look at our equation and see what information we have for the moment. The equation is more or less in the form of $y = ax^2 + bx + c$. To put it more clearly in this form (so we have no coefficient for y), divide both sides by the coefficient for y.

$$\frac{1}{4} \cdot 4y = 4x^2 + 16x - 24 \cdot \frac{1}{4}$$
$$y = x^2 + 4x - 6$$

Now you know that the parabola opens up because the squared term is x, and its coefficient is positive. The next step is to find the vertex and p. In order to do so, we need to put the equation into the other form; the one with the h's and the k's, which means rearranging it yet again and completing the square. First, move the number to the other side.

$$6 + y = x^2 + 4x - 6 + 6 \text{ becomes } 6 + y = x^2 + 4x$$

Then, complete the square of x.

$$y + 6 + 4 = x^2 + 4x + 4$$
$$y + 10 = (x + 2)^2$$

You can see that this is now in the form $(x - h)^2 = 4p(y - k)$. In the case of our particular equation, h is -2 and y is -10. So the vertex of the parabola is at $(-2, -10)$. We can also see that since the coefficient of $(y - k)$ is 1, $p = \frac{1}{4}$.

If the vertex is at $(-2, -10)$ and $p = \frac{1}{4}$, what is the focus? You know that the parabola opens upwards, and this means that the focus is p above the vertex, at the same x-coordinate. Move a distance of p, or $\frac{1}{4}$, above -10—the y-coordinate—and you find $(-2, -9\frac{3}{4})$. There's the focus.

What is its directrix? The directrix is the line p below the vertex, since we are dealing with a parabola that opens upwards. The vertex is $(-2, -10)$ and $\frac{1}{4}$ down we find the horizontal line $y = -10\frac{1}{4}$, and that's your directrix. And then, kid, you're in business. Here's what the parabola looks like when we sketch its graph using the focus, directrix, and the two easy points, $x = 0$ and $x = -4$.

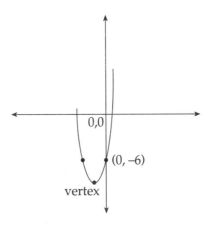

0,0

(0, –6)

vertex

EXERCISE 11.2

1. In what direction does the parabola with equation
$y = -x^2 + 4x - 10$ go? What is its vertex? What is its
directrix? Is it a function?

2. What is the equation of a parabola with vertex (2, 3)
and focus $(2, 3\frac{1}{4})$? Is it a function?

3. What is the equation of a parabola with vertex (1, 0)
and focus (2, 0)? Is it a function?

4. What are the directrix, vertex, and focus of a parabola
of equation $x = y^2 + 5x - 8$? In what direction does it
open? Is it a function?

5. What are the directrix, vertex, and focus of a parabola
of equation $y = x^2 + 8x - 20$? In what direction does
it open? Is it a function?

6. What are the directrix, vertex, and focus of a parabola
of equation $x = -\frac{1}{8}y^2$? In what direction does it open?
Is it a function?

7. What are the directrix, vertex, and focus of a parabola
of equation $x = -4y^2 + 8y - 9$? In what direction does
it open? Is it a function?

8. What are the directrix, vertex, and focus of a parabola
of equation $y = -x^2 + 6x + 10$? In what direction does
it open? Is it a function?

MORE ABOUT GRAPHING QUADRATIC EQUATIONS

Now that the graphical expression of a quadratic equation has been made clear, perhaps it has occurred to you that in your first introduction to quadratic equations they were set equal to 0 rather than to y. You remember $x^2 - 10x + 16 = 0$. What is an equation like this going to express in its graph?

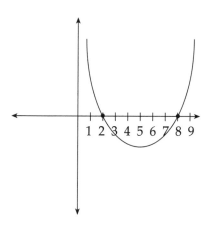

The formula for this particular parabola is $y = x^2 - 10x + 16$. As you know, the points at which the parabola intersects the x-axis are the points at which $y = 0$, and to find these you set the equation equal to 0, as in $0 = x^2 - 10x + 16$. After setting this equation equal to 0, you can factor it and get $0 = (x - 2)(x - 8)$, which gives you the roots of the equation, 2 and 8. Why would you want the roots? Because the roots of a quadratic equation give you additional information: They indicate the points at which the parabola intercepts the x-axis.

THE PERFECT SQUARE

If a parabola has the equation of a perfect square, what then? Say $y = x^2 - 6x + 9$. When the equation is set equal to 0 you can factor, so $0 = (x - 3)(x - 3)$. The information yielded is that this parabola touches the x-axis at only one point, $(3, 0)$, which is also its vertex, as you see when it's graphed.

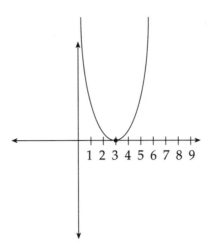

Y-INTERCEPTS AND ROOTS OF EQUATIONS

Setting a parabolic equation with its unsquared term equal to 0 works the same way for parabolas that open up sideways, and intersect with the y-axis, except that then you have the equation in terms of x.

$$x = y^2 + y - 6$$

You set the equation equal to 0 and then factor.

$$0 = y^2 + y - 6 \text{ becomes } 0 = (y + 3)(y - 2)$$

As you can see here, the parabola intersects the y-axis at the points $(0, 2)$ and $(0, -3)$.

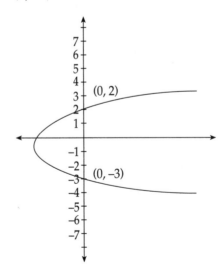

WHAT ABOUT EQUATIONS THAT DON'T FACTOR?

What about those equations that you can't factor? What about those equations that give imaginary roots when put into the quadratic formula? Clearly, the quadratic equations that give imaginary roots (remember your old friend i?) don't intersect the x-axis. That's why they don't have real roots at which $y = 0$. For instance, the equation $y = x^2 + 3x + 5$ can't be factored when put into the form of $0 = x^2 + 3x + 5$, and when you put it into the quadratic formula it yields a negative root, which is the product of an imaginary number. So, graph it, and see what sort of shape you get.

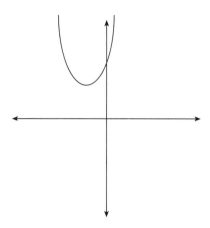

Notice that the parabola does not intersect the x-axis; that's why it doesn't yield any real number roots.

ISN'T THERE SOME OTHER WAY TO FIND OUT ABOUT ROOTS?

If you are resolutely opposed to factoring, there *is* some additional information about the equation's roots present in the equation itself. A parabola in the form $ax^2 + bx + c = y$ that yields roots by being set equal to 0 (as in $ax^2 + bx + c = 0$), says a number of things. One is something we discussed when you were learning how to complete the square in an equation: The second and third terms of the equation inform you about the roots. To put it simply, the sum of the roots of the equation is equal to $-\dfrac{b}{a}$, and the product of the roots of the equation is equal to $\dfrac{c}{a}$.

$$root_1 + root_2 = -\frac{b}{a}$$

$$root_1 root_2 = \frac{c}{a}$$

This information can make it easier for you to determine quickly whether a parabola has real or imaginary roots, and also if it is the product of a squared binomial and therefore has only one root.

The quadratic formula $\left(\dfrac{-b \pm \sqrt{b^2 - 4ac}}{2a}\right)$ also gives you a short-hand way to determine what type of roots an equation has. As you know, the reason a number is imaginary is that it's a square root of a negative number; thus, when the section of the quadratic equation that is under the square root sign is negative, you must have two imaginary roots.

$$b^2 - 4ac < 0 \text{ means two imaginary roots}$$

And when the section under the square root sign is equal to 0, you've got a perfect square, which means that there are two equal real roots, or only one intersection with the x-axis.

$$b^2 - 4ac = 0 \text{ means two equal real roots}$$

GRAPHING OTHER FUNCTIONS

Functions?! you say. Yes, as you know, the upside-down and right-side-up parabolas—the parabolas set equal to y—are functions of x and can be seen as $y = f(x) = ax^2 + bx + c$. Remember, a function has one, and only one, value of y for each value of x.

There are two other particular functions of x you should be familiar with: **radical functions** and **rational functions**.

Radical functions are functions which contain a radical sign, also known to you as a square root or root sign. For instance, the function $y = \sqrt{x}$ is a radical function. The graph of this function looks like this:

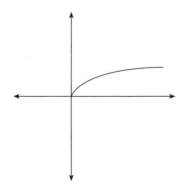

Notice that it looks almost like half of a sideways parabola; if the other half were there it would be the graph of $y^2 = x$, and not a function. It would certainly not pass the vertical line test, as you can see if you sketch in the other side.

A rational function, on the other hand, is a function that expresses the quotient of a polynomial. Remember, the term polynomial can also stand for a monomial; what is important here is that in these cases the function is expressed *as a quotient*. Some examples of rational functions are

$y = \dfrac{x^2 - 3x + 2}{x^2 - x}$, which can be factored to $\dfrac{(x-2)(x-1)}{x(x-1)}$, and then $\dfrac{(x-2)}{x}$; it can also be graphed:

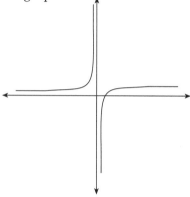

The graph of $y = \dfrac{1}{x}$ looks like this:

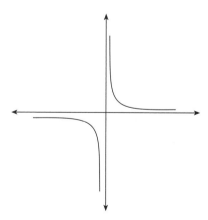

And one more rational function, $y = \dfrac{1}{x(x-2)}$, has a graph:

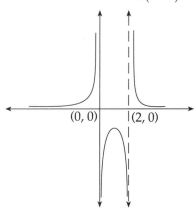

(0, 0)   (2, 0)

Notice that a lot of the graphs you draw and see look the same; they're just shifted around the coordinate system. If you pay close attention, you'll learn to recognize the different shapes of graphs, and what types of equations they correspond to.

Notice that for all of these functions, there comes a value or values at which the graph approaches infinity. This value corresponds to the number at which the equation approaches a denominator of 0. The lines at which this happens are called **asymptotes**, and you will see more of them when you advance further into mathematics. The vertical line set equal to x at which y approaches infinity, positive or negative, is called the **vertical asymptote**. The vertical asymptotes of the last graph above are the lines $x = 2$, and $x = 0$. These are the points at which the equation approaches a denominator of 0—a handy description of a vertical asymptote. The horizontal line set equal to y at which x approaches infinity, positive or negative, is called the **horizontal asymptote**. In the last graph above the horizontal asymptote is the line $y = 0$. Not every rational function has a horizontal asymptote.

TO GRAPH FUNCTIONS, YET AGAIN

You already know how to graph various equations by substituting in various values for the coordinates, plotting the points, and then forming the line. What you also need to be on the lookout for now are the asymptotes. When you're graphing a rational function, make sure you mark the vertical asymptote(s) on your sketch; other important points are the ones at which the equation *approaches* the asymptote(s)—if the asymptote is the line $x = 1$ make sure to mark the x-coordinates $\dfrac{1}{2}$ and $1\dfrac{1}{2}$—as well as the point at which $x = 0$ and the point at which $y = 0$, if you can. These points will give you a fairly clear beginning of a representative sketch.

Example

Graph the function $f(x) = \dfrac{x+4}{x+2}$ and give the vertical asymptote and, if applicable, the horizontal asymptote.

    The first thing you want to do when you have a rational function is to factor it, if possible. Since that isn't an option here, we'll move on to the graph. Essentially, you graph a rational function as you would graph any equation: Put in values for x and find the corresponding values for y, plot the points—particularly the smaller points on either side of the point at which the denominator of the function approaches 0, and the x and y-intercepts—and draw your lines.

    For instance, since the fraction gets a denominator of 0 when x equals –2, that means $x = -2$ is the vertical asymptote. Draw it in as a dotted line on your graph, and then start filling in the values for x that surround it. If $x = -1$, $y = 3$. If $x = -1\frac{1}{2}$, $y = 5$. If $x = -2\frac{1}{2}$, $y = -3$. If $x = -3$ then $y = -1$, and the y-intercept, if $x = 0$, $y = 2$, and the x-intercept $y = 0$, if $x = -4$. Just to cover all of the bases, when $x = 2$, $y = 1\frac{1}{2}$, and when $x = -6$, $y = \frac{1}{2}$. These points give you enough of an opportunity to sketch the graph.

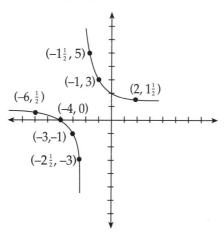

    Is there a horizontal asymptote here? Well, there appears to be a point at which the x approaches infinity and negative infinity: the line at which $y = 1$. So the horizontal asymptote is the line $y = 1$, and the vertical asymptote is the line $x = -2$.

ABSOLUTE FUNCTIONS

What if $f(x) = |x + 2|$, also known as the absolute value of x plus 2? Well, you'll soon be able to recognize absolute value functions. For one thing, no matter what x is, $f(x)$ is going to be positive. Beyond that, this one, at least, is linear, meaning straight lines rather than curved ones. So it's going to look like this:

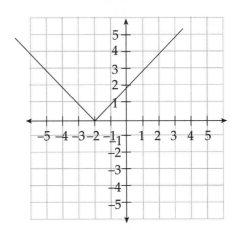

So if you ever see a V-shaped graph of a function that contains only positive or 0 values of y, you should be pretty sure you've got an absolute value function.

EXERCISE 11.3

1. Does the parabola $y = x^2 - 3x + 5$ have two real distinct roots, two real equal roots, or two imaginary roots? Is it a function?

2. Is the parabola $y = x^2 + 6x + 9$ a function? At what point, if any, does it intercept the x-axis?

3. What kind of shape occurs when $f(x) = x^2 - 3x + 2$ is graphed? Does the graph intersect the x-axis? Does it intersect the y-axis?

4. Graph the function $f(x) = \dfrac{x+1}{x-2}$. Is it a rational function or a radical function?

5. Does the function in question 5 have a horizontal asymptote? If so, what is it?

6. What is the vertical asymptote of the function in question 5?

7. If $f(x) = 3x^2 - 4x + 5$, what is the sum of its roots? What is the product of its roots? Are the two roots imaginary, distinct real roots, or equal real roots?

8. What is the vertical asymptote of $f(x) = \dfrac{1}{x^2}$?

ANSWERS TO CHAPTER ELEVEN EXERCISES

ANSWERS TO EXERCISE 11.1

1. Focus is $(0, 2)$; directrix is $y = -2$; it opens up; it is a function.

2. Focus is $(1, 0)$; directrix is $x = -1$; it opens to the right; it is not a function.

3. Focus is $(0, -\dfrac{1}{4})$; directrix is $y = \dfrac{1}{4}$; it opens down; it is a function.

4. $x^2 = 20y$; directrix is $y = -5$; it is a function.

5. Focus is $\left(-\dfrac{5}{16}, 0\right)$; directrix is $x = \dfrac{5}{16}$; it opens sideways to the left; it is not a function.

6. $x^2 = 8y$; directrix is $y = -2$; it is a function.

7. Focus is $(0, 2)$; directrix is $y = -2$; it opens up; it is a function.

8. Focus is $\left(\dfrac{1}{2}, 0\right)$; directrix is $x = -\dfrac{1}{2}$; it opens to the right; it is not a function.

ANSWERS TO EXERCISE 11.2

1. It opens down; vertex is $(-2, -14)$; directrix is $y = -13\dfrac{3}{4}$; it is a function.

2. $y - 3 = (x - 2)^2$; it is a function.

3. $y^2 = 4(x - 1)$; it is not a function.

4. Directrix is $x = 2\dfrac{1}{4}$; vertex is $(2, 0)$; focus is $\left(1\dfrac{3}{4}, 0\right)$; it opens to the left; it is not a function.

5. Directrix is $y = -36\frac{1}{4}$; vertex is $(-4, -36)$; focus is $(-4, -35\frac{3}{4})$; it opens up; it is a function.

6. Directrix is $x = 2$; focus is $(-2, 0)$; it opens to the left; it is not a function.

7. Directrix is $x = -12\frac{7}{8}$; vertex is $(-13, -1)$; focus $= (-13\frac{1}{8}, -1)$; it opens to the left; it is not a function.

8. Directrix is $y = 1\frac{1}{4}$; vertex is $(-3, 1)$; focus is $(-3, \frac{3}{4})$; it opens down; it is a function.

ANSWERS TO EXERCISE 11.3

1. Two imaginary roots; it is a function.

2. It is a function; it touches on the x-axis at $x = -3$ only.

3. A parabola that opens up; it intersects the x-axis at points $(-1, 0)$ and $(-2, 0)$; it intercepts the y-axis at point $(2, 0)$.

4. 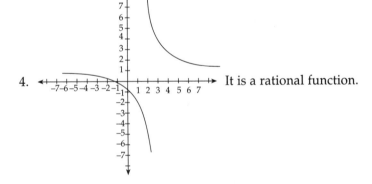 It is a rational function.

5. Its horizontal asymptote is the line $y = 1$.

6. Its vertical asymptote is the line $x = 2$.

7. The sum of its roots is $\frac{4}{3}$; the product of its roots is $\frac{5}{3}$; the roots are imaginary.

8. The vertical asymptote is the line 0.

CHAPTER 12

Other Conics

Why the heck is a parabola called a *conic* anyway? Well, because it's formed, in a sense, by slicing up a cone. That's the way all conic sections are originally formed, at least conceptually. As we've said before, there are other conics besides the parabola. The angle at which the cone is sliced determines what type of conic it is. Take a look.

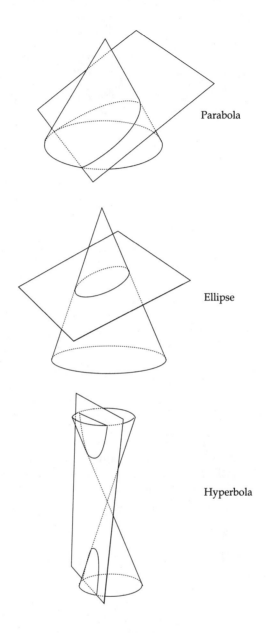

Parabola

Ellipse

Hyperbola

Each has a particular ratio of distance from two fixed points, just as a parabola has its one-to-one ratio distance from its focus and directrix.

ELLIPSES

An **ellipse** is a type of conic that looks something like a squashed circle.

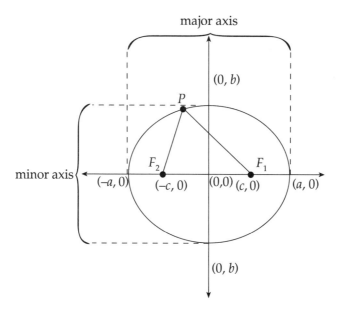

For any point P on the ellipse, the distances between that point and the two **foci** (we'll call them F_1 and F_2) always add up to a constant sum. Foci is the plural of focus.

There are two additional measures in an ellipse: the **major axis**—the line through the foci of the ellipse the long way, with a length of $2a$, and the **minor axis**—the line through the center of the ellipse and perpendicular to the major axis, with a length of $2b$. All the information and equations presented here refer to ellipses located on the origin of the coordinate system.

HOW WE DERIVE THE EQUATION FOR AN ELLIPSE

The way the equation for an ellipse is determined is by the definition of an ellipse: For any point P on the ellipse where PF_1 is the distance between P and F_1, and PF_2 is the distance between P and F_2, $PF_1 + PF_2 = 2a$. Thus, the distance formula can be called into action just as it was with the parabola, and the equation, after simplification, becomes $\dfrac{x^2}{a^2} + \dfrac{y^2}{b^2} = 1$ as long as $a > b$. The a and the b represent what they do in the diagram: a is the distance from the origin to the edge of the ellipse along the major axis, and b is the distance from the origin to the edge of the ellipse along the minor axis. The points $(a, 0)$ and $(-a, 0)$ are called the vertices of the ellipse. You can also rearrange this equation (by multiplying it all by a^2b^2) to say that the equation of an ellipse whose major axis is on the x-axis is $b^2x^2 + a^2y^2 = a^2b^2$.

If the ellipse has its major axis on the y-axis, then the equation is

$$\frac{x^2}{b^2} + \frac{y^2}{a^2} = 1 \text{ or } b^2y^2 + a^2x^2 = a^2b^2.$$

How can you tell which type of ellipse you're dealing with when the a's and b's are replaced by numbers? By ellipse definition, $a > b$, so whichever denominator is larger defines whether that denominator is a or b.

Example

$\dfrac{x^2}{16} + \dfrac{y^2}{9} = 1$ represents an ellipse with its major axis along which axis?

Essentially the question is asking whether the ellipse is in the form $\dfrac{x^2}{a^2} + \dfrac{y^2}{b^2} = 1$ or $\dfrac{x^2}{b^2} + \dfrac{y^2}{a^2} = 1$. Since $a > b$ in an ellipse, and $16 > 9$, this is an ellipse that has its major axis along the x-axis.

ECCENTRICITY

Another important variable in an ellipse is c; c represents the distance from the origin to either foci of the ellipse.

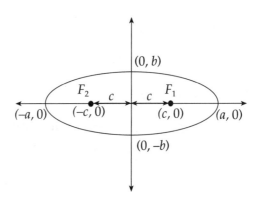

Why does this matter? Because one of the measures of all these conics is eccentricity, or e. Eccentricity represents the thinness of a shape; a long, narrow ellipse has a greater value of e than a short, fat one. The eccentricity of an ellipse is given as $e = \dfrac{c}{a}$. The eccentricity of this ellipse is $\dfrac{\sqrt{7}}{4}$.

SOME ELLIPSE FACTS

Take a look at the triangle formed inside this ellipse by the distance from the origin to one of the foci and the distance from the origin to b.

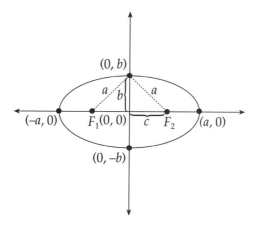

You already know these distances as b and c, and you know that the sum of the distances from any point on the ellipse to the foci is $2a$. The point $(0, b)$ on the y-axis is halfway between the foci, and the sum of its distances from both of the foci is $2a$. So the distance between $(0, b)$ and one of the foci is exactly half of $2a$, or a.

Since the triangle's vertex is at the origin, which is a perpendicular, you have a right triangle. This means that if you have two of the measures of the ellipse you can find the third with the Pythagorean Theorem, though be aware that the letters for the legs of the triangle are in different order. As you can see here, $b^2 + c^2 = a^2$. Still, it's pretty cool.

Example

For an ellipse with equation $\dfrac{x^2}{16} + \dfrac{y^2}{9} = 1$ find the vertices, the major axis, the minor axis, the foci, and the eccentricity.

Whew! A long list, but not to worry, it isn't hard. First, look at the denominators. The denominator of x is greater than the denominator of y; remember that the equations say that $a > b$. So we have an equation that's in the form $\dfrac{x^2}{a^2} + \dfrac{y^2}{b^2} = 1$, which is an ellipse on the x-axis. Now, let's evaluate the information. Since $a^2 = 16$, $a = 4$, and since $b^2 = 9$, $b = 3$. Now you know the vertices, which are a distance of a from the origin to the edges. Since $a = 4$, the vertices are $(4, 0)$ and $(-4, 0)$.

The variable a also gives us the sum of the distances—$2a$—from any point on the ellipse to the two foci, and this also gives us the measure of the distance across the ellipse, also known as the major axis. This distance is 8.

The minor axis is b away from the origin. Since b is 3, the span of the minor axis is $2b$, or 6.

You're almost there; now all you need are the foci themselves, and the eccentricity. Here's where that triangle comes in; you know that in this particular triangle, $b^2 + c^2 = a^2$ (look at the preceding diagram to get comfortable with these variables in this order). This means that $9 + c^2 = 16$, so, $c^2 = 7$, so $c = \sqrt{7}$. Thus, the foci are $(\sqrt{7}, 0)$ and $(-\sqrt{7}, 0)$. And the eccentricity, $\dfrac{c}{a}$, is $\dfrac{\sqrt{7}}{4}$. Nicely done.

EXERCISE 12.1

1. The ellipse $\dfrac{x^2}{9} + \dfrac{y^2}{25} = 1$ lies on which axis?

2. What are the vertices and the major and minor axis lengths of the ellipse in question 1?

3. What are the foci and the eccentricity of the ellipse in question 1?

4. Draw the graph of the ellipse in question 1.

5. The major axis of the ellipse $16x^2 + 25y^2 = 400$ lies on which axis?

6. What are the vertices and the major and minor axis lengths of the ellipse in question 5?

7. What are the foci and the eccentricity of the ellipse in question 5?

8. Draw the graph of the ellipse in question 5.

MORE CONICS: HYPERBOLAS

Guess what: **Hyperbolas** are conics that have a set relationship to two fixed points, $(-c, 0)$ and $(c, 0)$, which are also known as foci. Big surprise. But, instead of being like ellipses, whose points have the same sum of the distances to the two foci, hyperbolas have this quality: The *difference* of the distances between every point on a hyperbola and its two foci is the same.

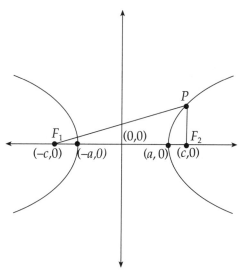

In the diagram, no matter where a point P is on the hyperbola, the difference between the distance from it to $(c, 0)$ and the distance from it to $(-c, 0)$ is the same. Again, the hyperbolas we're talking about here are those that are centered on the origin.

We are going to call the vertices of these curves—the points at which they are closest to each other—$(a, 0)$ and $(-a, 0)$. This allows us to define the difference between any point P on the hyperbola and the two foci as $2a$. Take a look at the diagram so you can see how this makes sense; if you subtract the distance between the vertex $(a, 0)$ to the focus $(c, 0)$ from the distance between that same point (the vertex), and the other focus $(-c, 0)$, you are left with the space between the two vertices, or $2a$. Thus, where PF_1 is the distance between P and F_1, and PF_2 is the distance between P and F_2,

$PF_1 - PF_2 = 2a$ and, by putting this information into the distance formula and simplifying it, we get the equation for a hyperbola, $\frac{x^2}{a^2} - \frac{y^2}{b^2} = 1$. Looks a whole lot like the formula for an ellipse, but here we're dealing with a difference instead of a sum. You may be asking yourself, where the heck is the b in a hyperbola, and what is its function? Well, the b is on the other axis from the foci, and in addition to being part of the overall equation for the hyperbola, it provides other useful information; it defines the hyperbola's asymptotes. The asymptotes occur at the lines $y = \frac{b}{a}x$ and $y = -\frac{b}{a}x$. As you can imagine, these lines are wonderfully helpful when graphing hyperbolas. The easiest way to plot the lines on your hyperbola graph is to draw a box, using $y = b$ and $-b$ and $x = a$ and $-a$ as its borders. This way $y = \frac{b}{a}x$ and $y = -\frac{b}{a}x$—the asymptotes—form its diagonals.

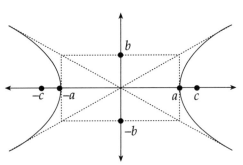

How does one find the foci of a hyperbola from the equation? Well, $c^2 = a^2 + b^2$, because you can draw a triangle in a hyperbola just as you can in an ellipse.

Example

What are the vertices, the foci, and the asymptotes of the hyperbola with equation $\frac{x^2}{25} - \frac{y^2}{16} = 1$? While you're at it, draw the graph of this hyperbola.

To answer these questions, we need to evaluate the information given in the equation. Clearly you have a hyperbola in the form of $\frac{x^2}{a^2} - \frac{y^2}{b^2} = 1$, where $a^2 = 25$, and $b^2 = 16$. The vertices are at $(a, 0)$ and $(-a, 0)$ which makes them $(5, 0)$ and $(-5, 0)$.

Next, the foci. Foci are $(c, 0)$ and $(-c, 0)$ and, as you know, $c^2 = a^2 + b^2$. So, $c^2 = 25 + 16$, and $c^2 = 41$, so $c = \sqrt{41}$, and the foci are $(\sqrt{41}, 0)$ and $(-\sqrt{41}, 0)$.

Now the asymptotes; asymptotes are the lines $y = \dfrac{b}{a}x$ and $y = -\dfrac{b}{a}x$, so you can enter your values for a and b and be done with it. After substituting, you'll see that the lines at which x approaches infinity on the hyperbola are at $y = \dfrac{4}{5}$ and $y = -\dfrac{4}{5}$.

You've answered the questions, now you must sketch the hyperbola. Put a, b, and an approximation for c on your graph. An approximation for c would take into account that the square root of 36 is 6, and the square root of 49 is 7, so the square root of 41 is somewhere between those two.

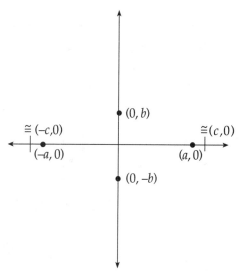

Now, to sketch in the asymptotes, construct the central box of $x = a$ and $x = -a$, and $y = b$ and $y = -b$, and then draw in the diagonals, which are the asymptotes of your graph. Then, using $(a, 0)$ and $(-a, 0)$ as the vertices, sketch the hyperbola.

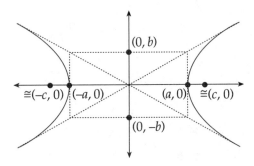

That's all there is to it.

What if you see a hyperbola presented as an equation $\dfrac{y^2}{a^2} - \dfrac{x^2}{b^2} = 1$?

As you might imagine, a hyperbola with an equation like this has its vertices on the y-axis rather than the x-axis. Other than its orientation, it has the same coordinates as any other hyperbola: Its vertices are marked by a, in this case $(0, a)$ and $(0, -a)$, and its asymptotes are the lines $y = \dfrac{a}{b}x$ and $y = \dfrac{a}{b}-x$. Its foci are $(0, c)$ and $(0, -c)$, and happily, the equation $c^2 = a^2 + b^2$ holds true here as well.

Try some questions about hyperbolas on your own.

EXERCISE 12.2

1. On which axis is the hyperbola $\dfrac{x^2}{9} - \dfrac{y^2}{16} = 1$?

2. What are the vertices, asymptotes, and foci of the hyperbola in question 1?

3. Sketch the graph of the hyperbola in question 1.

4. What is the equation of the hyperbola with vertices $(2, 0)$ and $(-2, 0)$ and foci $\left(\sqrt{5},0\right)$ and $\left(-\sqrt{5},0\right)$?

5. What are the asymptotes of the hyperbola in question 4?

6. What is the equation of the hyperbola with vertices $(0, 3)$ and $(0, -3)$, and asymptotes $y = \dfrac{3}{4}x$ and $y = -\dfrac{3}{4}x$?

7. Sketch the graph of the hyperbola in question 6.

8. What are the vertices of the hyperbola with foci $(0, 5)$ and $(0, -5)$, and asymptotes $y = \frac{4}{3}x$ and $y = -\frac{4}{3}x$?

ANSWERS TO CHAPTER TWELVE EXERCISES

ANSWERS TO EXERCISE 12.1

1. The y-axis.

2. The vertices are $(0, 5)$ and $(0, -5)$, major axis = 10, minor axis = 6.

3. The foci are $(0, 4)$ and $(0, -4)$, and the eccentricity is $\frac{4}{5}$.

4.

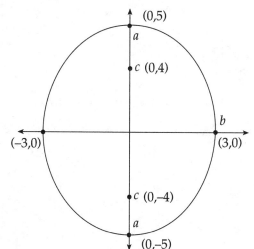

5. The x-axis (divide both sides by 400 to find the more familiar expression, or look at it as $b^2x^2 + a^2y^2 = a^2b^2$ because $a > b$).

6. The vertices are $(5, 0)$ and $(-5, 0)$, the major axis is 10, and the minor axis is 8.

7. The foci are (3, 0) and (–3, 0), and the eccentricity is $\frac{3}{5}$.

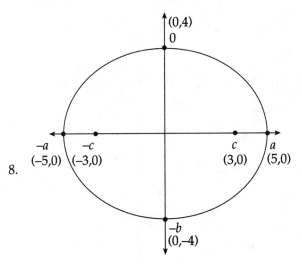

8.

ANSWERS TO EXERCISE 12.2

1. The x-axis.

2. The vertices are (3, 0) and (–3, 0), the asymptotes are $y = \frac{4}{3}x$ and $y = -\frac{4}{3}x$, and the foci are (5, 0) and (–5, 0).

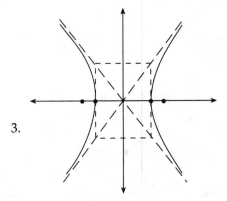

3.

4. The equation is $\frac{x^2}{4} - y^2 = 1$.

5. The asymptotes are $y = \dfrac{1}{2}x$ and $y = -\dfrac{1}{2}x$

6. The equation is $\dfrac{y^2}{9} - \dfrac{x^2}{16} = 1.$

7.

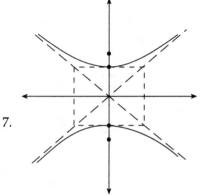

8. The vertices are $(0, 4)$ and $(0, -4)$, and they are along the y-axis just as the foci are.

Trigonometry

CHAPTER 13

Trigonometry of Degrees

A right triangle with two sides 3 and 4 and an unknown hypotenuse presents no real mystery about the measure of its unlabeled side; the Pythagorean Theorem can provide the missing information. And a right triangle with the measure for one other angle filled in—well, it's easy to find the third angle from the rule of 180. But what can you do with a right triangle whose angle measurements you know, that gives only one side's measure and asks you for the other two? Or gives only the measures of the sides, and asks you for the measure of the angles? Here is the first of many instances in which **trigonometry** can come to your rescue. Yes, that's "trig" to those of us in the know, which now includes you. The word trigonometry means, essentially, the measuring of triangles, and indeed, measuring triangles is the first thing we'll do. The further you go in other areas of pure or applied mathematics—architecture, physics, harmonics—the more useful and powerful trigonometry will prove to be.

THE TRIGONOMETRIC RATIOS

Remember similar triangles? What made them similar was the ratio of their sides, and the equivalence of their angles. (Triangles in trigonometry are labeled by their vertices—the angles denoted in capital letters—and the sides opposite those angles are named by the same letter but lower case.)

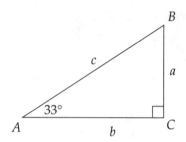

For a right triangle ABC with sides a, b, and c and angles A, B, and C, the triangle made by extending b and c to form a right triangle further out must be similar to ABC.

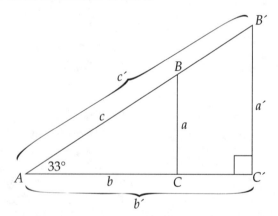

This means that the ratios of the sides must be equal; $\frac{a}{b}$ for the first triangle is equal to $\frac{a'}{b'}$ for the second triangle. This holds true for the ratio of all the sides, $\frac{c}{b} = \frac{c'}{b'}$, and so on. As long as the triangles are similar (which means that their corresponding angles are equal), no matter how large or small they become, the ratios of their corresponding sides are going to be equal. What we can deduce from this is that the ratio of the sides depends upon the size of the angle. Another way to say this, mathematically, is that the ratio of the sides is a function of the angle. So the ratio of sides $\frac{a}{c}$, for instance, will always be equal for all similar triangles; the ratio we have for the particular triangle in question will be equal for all right triangles in which angle A measures 33 degrees.

We call this particular function of the angle—with the measure of the side opposite the angle over the measure of the hypotenuse—the sine function. Sine means $\dfrac{\text{opposite}}{\text{hypotenuse}}$. That is what sine represents for right triangles (don't worry, we'll get to non-right triangles soon enough), and, as you can see from the explanation thus far, a specific numerical ratio exists for the sine of every possible angle. The sine for angle A, which is 33 degrees, is commonly expressed as sin 33° or sin A, and it is 0.5446. Happily, you do not have to go through the process of measuring the sides in question and dividing them out; you will always be presented with a table of the values of their various trigonometric angles and functions. We will address those tables in a moment. First, what did we mean by saying "their various functions?"

The sine is not the only trigonometric function; there are six basic functions of each angle; they depend on the three sides of a triangle in relation to the angle in question—the opposite side, the adjacent side, and the hypotenuse.

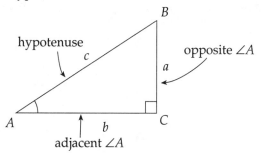

The functions are defined as follows, and given for angle A in triangle ABC.

$$\text{sine or sin} = \frac{opp}{hyp}; \ \ \sin\ A = \frac{a}{c}$$

$$\text{cosine or cos} = \frac{adj}{hyp}; \ \ \cos\ A = \frac{b}{c}$$

$$\text{tangent or tan} = \frac{opp}{adj}; \ \ \tan\ A = \frac{a}{b}$$

$$\text{cosecant or csc} = \frac{hyp}{opp}; \ \ \csc\ A = \frac{c}{a}$$

$$\text{secant or sec} = \frac{hyp}{adj}; \quad \sec A = \frac{c}{b}$$

$$\text{cotangent or cot} = \frac{adj}{opp}; \quad \cot A = \frac{b}{a}$$

EXERCISE 13.1

1. For triangle ABC, $\sin B$ is $\frac{b}{c}$. What are the other five trigonometric functions of $\angle B$?

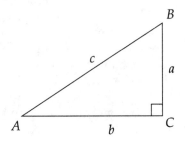

2. For triangle ABC, $\cos B$ is $\frac{7}{\sqrt{130}}$, or $\frac{7\sqrt{130}}{130}$ when its denominator is rationalized. What are the other five trigonometric functions of $\angle B$?

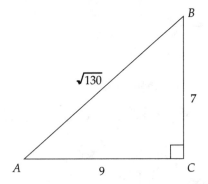

3. For triangle ABC, what is sin B?

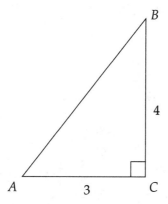

4. For the triangle above, which is larger, sin A or sin B?

5. For the triangle in question 3, which is larger, cos B or sin A?

6. For the triangle in question 3, which is larger, tan B or tan A?

7. For the triangle in question 3, which is larger, cot A or cot B?

8. For the triangle in question 3, which is larger, csc A or sec B?

TABLES

We've said that tables of the trigonometric functions will be available to you, in printed form as well as programmed into your calculator. But how do you use them?

x	sin (x)	cos (x)	tan (x)	cot (x)	sec (x)	csc (x)	
0°	.0000	1.0000	.0000	. . . .	1.000	. . . .	90°
1°	.0175	.9998	.0175	57.29	1.000	57.30	89°
2°	.0349	.9994	.0349	28.64	1.001	28.65	88°
3°	.0523	.9986	.0524	19.08	1.001	19.11	87°
4°	.0698	.9976	.0699	14.30	1.002	14.34	86°
5°	.0872	.9962	.0875	11.43	1.004	11.47	85°
6°	.1045	.9945	.1051	9.514	1.006	9.567	84°
7°	.1219	.9925	.1228	8.144	1.008	8.206	83°
8°	.1392	.9903	.1405	7.115	1.010	7.185	82°
9°	.1564	.9877	.1584	6.314	1.012	6.392	81°
10°	.1736	.9848	.1763	5.671	1.015	5.759	80°
11°	.1908	.9816	.1944	5.145	1.019	5.241	79°
12°	.2079	.9781	.2126	4.705	1.022	4.810	78°
13°	.2250	.9744	.2309	4.331	1.026	4.445	77°
14°	.2419	.9703	.2493	4.011	1.031	4.134	76°
15°	.2588	.9659	.2679	3.732	1.035	3.864	75°
16°	.2756	.9613	.2867	3.487	1.040	3.628	74°
17°	.2924	.9563	.3057	3.271	1.046	3.420	73°
18°	.3090	.9511	.3249	3.078	1.051	3.236	72°
19°	.3256	.9455	.3443	2.904	1.058	3.072	71°
20°	.3420	.9397	.3640	2.747	1.064	2.924	70°
21°	.3584	.9336	.3839	2.605	1.071	2.790	69°
22°	.3746	.9272	.4040	2.475	1.079	2.669	68°
23°	.3907	.9205	.4245	2.356	1.086	2.559	67°
24°	.4067	.9135	.4452	2.246	1.095	2.459	66°
25°	.4226	.9063	.4663	2.145	1.103	2.366	65°
26°	.4384	.8988	.4877	2.050	1.113	2.281	64°
27°	.4540	.8910	.5095	1.963	1.122	2.203	63°
28°	.4695	.8829	.5317	1.881	1.133	2.130	62°
29°	.4848	.8746	.5543	1.804	1.143	2.063	61°
30°	.5000	.8660	.5774	1.732	1.155	2.000	60°
31°	.5150	.8572	.6009	1.664	1.167	1.942	59°
32°	.5299	.8480	.6249	1.600	1.179	1.887	58°
33°	.5446	.8387	.6494	1.540	1.192	1.836	57°
34°	.5592	.8290	.6745	1.483	1.206	1.788	56°
35°	.5736	.8192	.7002	1.428	1.221	1.743	55°
36°	.5878	.8090	.7265	1.376	1.236	1.701	54°
37°	.6018	.7986	.7536	1.327	1.252	1.662	53°
38°	.6157	.7880	.7813	1.280	1.269	1.624	52°
39°	.6293	.7771	.8098	1.235	1.287	1.589	51°
40°	.6428	.7660	.8391	1.192	1.305	1.556	50°
41°	.6561	.7547	.8693	1.150	1.325	1.524	49°
42°	.6691	.7431	.9004	1.111	1.346	1.494	48°
43°	.6820	.7314	.9325	1.072	1.367	1.466	47°
44°	.6947	.7193	.9657	1.036	1.390	1.440	46°
45°	.7071	.7071	1.000	1.000	1.414	1.414	45°
	cos (x)	sin (x)	cot (x)	tan (x)	csc (x)	sec (x)	x

To find the value of any of the six basic trigonometric functions of a particular angle that you have a measure for in degrees, look up the angle on the left side of the table, for instance, 33°, the angle A that started off this chapter. Then look at the top of the table until you find the function you need. The sin A for when $\frac{A}{n} = 33°$ is .5446.

You may have noticed, you clever thing, you, that the table appears to go up only to 45 degrees. If you look to the right side of the table, you'll find the angles above 45° going from the bottom of the table to the top. How can this be? You might have some idea, because you just finished exercise 13.1.

In a right triangle, the two acute angles must be complementary, according to the rule of 180. And, in a right triangle, the functions of the two acute angles are related. In right triangle ABC, sin A is $\frac{a}{c}$, the side opposite the angle in question, over the hypotenuse. What is also true is that cos B is also $\frac{a}{c}$, only in this case this represents the side that's adjacent to the angle in question, over the hypotenuse. As you can see, every function of A is equal to a different function of B.

$$\sin A = \frac{a}{c} = \cos B$$

$$\cos A = \frac{b}{c} = \sin B$$

$$\tan A = \frac{a}{b} = \cot B$$

$$\csc A = \frac{c}{a} = \sec B$$

$$\sec A = \frac{c}{b} = \csc B$$

$$\cot A = \frac{b}{a} = \tan B$$

The terrifically helpful thing about this is that since the acute angles must be complementary, if $\angle A$ is 60°, you know two things. One is that $\angle B$ must be 30° because of the rule of 180, and the other is that sin A is equal to cos B, and while sin 60° is not on the table, cos 30° is. The tables have even put this into shorthand for you; look up the right side to 60°, then move along to the *bottom* of the column that the chart calls sine; there you'll find the sine of 60°. You didn't even have to look at the top of the chart to first see that it is the cosine of 30°.

TO WORK ON A CALCULATOR

Most calculators have both degree modes and radian modes. Check your calculator's instructions to find out how to set it to degree mode, then enter the angle measure as a number, for instance, 30 for 30°, and press the key that corresponds to the correct function.

ANGLE MEASURES

You can see that an accurate measure of an angle is particularly important to trigonometry and all of the trigonometric tables. In light of this, we'll present another measurement of angles in order to allow you to be even more exact. Angles have thus far been measured in degrees. What you didn't know is that each degree is made up of 60 minutes. An angle that before you might have called "25 and a half degrees," you may now call 25 degrees and 30 minutes, or 25° 30'. To find the value of this on the trigonometric function table, find, for example, sin 25° and sin 26°. These are .4226 and .4384 respectively. Subtract the smaller number from the larger one to find the one degree difference.

$$\begin{array}{r} .4384 \\ - \underline{.4226} \\ .0158 \end{array}$$

This is the difference in the sine function in jumping the one degree from 25° to 26°. Since 30 minutes equals one half of one degree, we take half of .0158, or .0079. Add this to the value of sin 25° and you have .4226 + .0079 = .4305, which is sin 25°30'. This method is called **interpolation**, and you won't have to deal with it if you have a calculator with trigonometric functions. If you do have such a calculator, simply convert minutes into fractions of degrees by dividing the number of minutes by 60 so you get a decimal, and then enter the complete decimal, in this case, 25.5, and press the appropriate function. This is a much more pleasant option.

Please note that when we interpolated with the table for the sine function here, we *added* the fractional minutes. For functions that decrease as the angle gets larger, you may need to subtract the fractional part. Simply look at the values on either side if you forget if it decreases or increases, or remember what the ratio stands for, and see whether it will increase or decrease as the angle itself increases.

EXERCISE 13.2

Use a calculator or the table provided on page 194 to find the following values; calculate out to the second place.

1. What is sin 27°?

2. What is cos 63°?

3. What is cot 24°40'?

4. What is csc 45°?

5. What is sec 45°20'?

6. What is tan 70°?

7. What is $\dfrac{\sin 30°}{\cos 30°}$?

8. What is tan 30°?

SOLVING RIGHT TRIANGLES WITH TRIGONOMETRIC FUNCTIONS

In trigonometry, to solve a right triangle means to identify the measures of all of its angles and all of its sides. This is your first practical application of trigonometric functions. How do you solve a right triangle in which ∠B = 24° and c = 35?

Well, when you know one angle besides the right angle of a triangle, you know the third angle by the rule of 180. Since ∠B is 24° and the right angle, c, is 90°, the remaining angle measures 66°. As for the sides, since you have one side and since really, trigonometry depends on ratios, you have them all. For instance, ∠B is 24°, and you have the length of the hypotenuse, so the sine of B is the length of the opposite side over the length of the hypotenuse, or $\dfrac{b}{35}$.

The sine of 24° can be found in the table; it is .4067. So, .4067 = $\dfrac{b}{35}$. Solve for b. You get 14.23. Now you can use the Pythagorean Theorem to find the third side, or you can use another trig function. The cosine of B is adjacent side over hypotenuse, or $\dfrac{a}{35}$, and cos 24° is .9135. So .9135 = $\dfrac{a}{35}$, so a = 31.97. Pretty nifty.

The function you use will depend on what information you are given. The more familiar you become with the various functions and their interrelationships, the more flexible and creative you will become in finding solutions.

UPS AND DOWNS

One of the ways these right triangle problems might be disguised (or practically applied, depending on your point of view), is in the form of a problem existing in the real world. For instance, a problem will tell you about a lighthouse (math tests love lighthouses), a surveyor (they love surveyors even more) and the angle of elevation. Here's how it might look: *A surveyor is studying a lighthouse. The lighthouse is perpendicular to the ground and is 700 feet high, and the angle of elevation to the light house is 35°. How far is the surveyor from the center of the base lighthouse?* These questions will often be accompanied by diagrams.

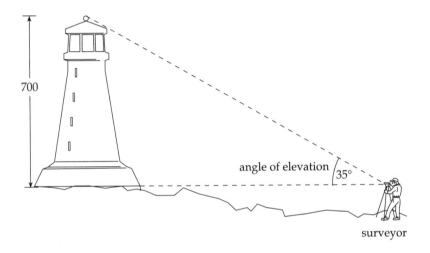

700

angle of elevation

35°

surveyor

The angle of elevation is exactly what it looks like here: The angle made from the viewer's eye to an object above the viewer. The angle of depression is the same thing, except it applies when the object is below the viewer's eye.

How far *is* the surveyor's viewing point from the base of the lighthouse, anyway? Well, the opposite side from the angle of elevation is 700. And the angle is 35°. The distance asked for represents the length of the side adjacent to the angle. Cotangent looks like a pretty good function to use here because it's the adjacent side over the opposite side: $\cot 35° = 1.428 = \dfrac{a}{700}$. Solve for a (the adjacent side) and you get $a = 999.6$, which is how many feet the surveyor's viewing point is from the base of the lighthouse. How many feet is his viewing point from the top of the lighthouse? That's the hypotenuse, and you can use the Pythagorean Theorem, or, since we're in the trig neighborhood, how about cosecant instead? That's hypotenuse over opposite. So, csc B = csc $35° = 1.743 = \dfrac{c}{700}$. Solve for c and you find that $c = 1{,}220.1$. And that's how far the top of the lighthouse is from the surveyor's viewing point.

EXERCISE 13.3

In questions one through five, the right angle is C.

1. Solve the right triangle ABC if $\angle A = 28°$ and side $b = 14$.

2. Solve the right triangle ABC if $\angle B = 28°$ and side $b = 22$.

3. Solve the right triangle ABC if $\angle A = 39°$ and side $c = 30$.

4. Solve the right triangle ABC if $\angle B = 40°$ and side $a = 20$.

5. Solve the right triangle ABC if $\angle B = 45°$ and side $c = 70$.

6. A dog is looking up at a balloon directly overhead, and a girl 40 feet away is looking up at the same balloon with an angle of elevation of 50°. The girl's viewing point is exactly horizontal to the dog's. How far above the dog is the balloon?

7. A boy on a highway overpass is planning to spit on his older sister's car. He spots it, stuck in traffic, at an angle of depression from the bridge of 37°. The overpass is 25 feet directly above the highway. How far is his sister's car from being directly under the overpass?

8. A student is planning to escape from an assembly by stretching a rope from the window out to the first available landing space, which is just beyond a shark-filled moat. The window of the assembly room is 50 feet above the ground, and the angle of elevation from the first available landing spot beyond the shark-filled moat to the window is 31°. How long must the rope be?

SPECIAL RIGHT TRIANGLES

You may remember special right triangles from the regular old pedestrian geometry section—how long ago it all seems! At any rate, you learned that for an isosceles right triangle, the sides are in the ratio of 1 to 1 to $\sqrt{2}$. The way this was discovered, though we neglected to mention it at the time, was by the Pythagorean Theorem. Since the sides were equal, you had $x^2 + x^2 = c^2$, so $2x^2 = c^2$, and by taking the square root of the sides, $x\sqrt{2} = c$. For the 30:60:90 right triangle we find the ratios of the lengths of the sides by first dividing an equilateral triangle in half by drawing a perpendicular. This creates two 30:60:90 right triangles, both with base $\dfrac{x}{2}$, hypotenuse x, and from the Pythagorean Theorem, middle length side $\dfrac{x}{2}\sqrt{3}$.

Why do we bring these things up now? Because the trigonometric values of the angles in these particular triangles are going to be very important to you as you go further down the mathematical road, and you should learn these values—dare we say it?—by heart. And by the way, you can also easily remember them by just thinking of the side ratios and then using them to make the function ratios yourself.

	sin	cos	tan
30°	$\dfrac{1}{2}$	$\dfrac{\sqrt{3}}{2}$	$\dfrac{1}{\sqrt{3}}$ or $\dfrac{\sqrt{3}}{3}$
60°	$\dfrac{\sqrt{3}}{2}$	$\dfrac{1}{2}$	$\sqrt{3}$
45°	$\dfrac{1}{\sqrt{2}}$ or $\dfrac{\sqrt{2}}{2}$	$\dfrac{1}{\sqrt{2}}$ or $\dfrac{\sqrt{2}}{2}$	1

What about the other three functions? You may have realized by now that the other functions are simply the reciprocal of the first three functions. Cosecant is the reciprocal of sine, secant is the reciprocal of cosine, and cotangent is the reciprocal of tangent. So to find those values for the special right triangles, just invert the reciprocal functions. One more important interrelationship: Just as tangent is opposite over adjacent, it can also be expressed as sine over cosine. This means, of course, that cotangent can be expressed as cosine over sine.

Here are the relationships:

$$\text{cosecant or } \csc = \frac{1}{\sin}$$

$$\text{secant or } \sec = \frac{1}{\cos}$$

$$\text{cotangent or } \cot = \frac{1}{\tan}$$

$$\cot = \frac{\cos}{\sin}$$

$$\tan = \frac{\sin}{\cos}$$

NON-RIGHT TRIANGLES

You're probably grumbling to yourself right about now that trigonometry is all very well for right triangles, but what about every other triangle in the world? Even if you weren't grumbling to yourself about this, here's where those non-right triangles come to the fore. The way trigonometry deals with non-right triangles is by recognizing that all triangles can be divided into two right triangles. Of course, you don't want to spend your time dividing triangles up and working through their parts every time, and happily some alternative methods exist. These alternative methods rely on the ways in which trigonometric functions interrelate. The most important of these interrelationships (and by most important we mean most helpful to you), are the **law of sines**, the **law of cosines**, and the **law of tangents**.

THE LAWS

As we've said, a triangle can be divided into two triangles that both contain right angles. Take a look at an ordinary triangle with height h.

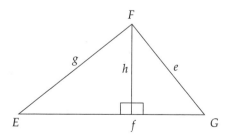

If we look at the two smaller triangles instead of looking at the whole triangle, we can see that sin $E = \dfrac{h}{g}$, and sin $G = \dfrac{h}{e}$. Solve both sides in terms of the height and you get $h = g$ sin E, and $h = e$ sin G. Thus, g sin E = e sin G. We can express this also as $\dfrac{\sin E}{e} = \dfrac{\sin G}{g}$. You could draw a perpendicular from the other vertices of the original triangle as well, and go through the same process, and this would always hold true. All of this yields the Law of Sines: For any triangle, the ratio of its angles' sines to their opposite sides is always equal. In other words, for any triangle ABC, $\dfrac{\sin A}{a} = \dfrac{\sin B}{b} = \dfrac{\sin C}{c}$.

Related to this is the Law of Cosines. The proof will have to wait, for now, but the law is as follows: For any triangle ABC, $c^2 = a^2 + b^2 - 2ab \cos C$. This holds true for any side of the triangle. So, $a^2 = b^2 + c^2 - 2bc \cos A$, and $b^2 = a^2 + c^2 - 2ac \cos B$.

How do these laws help you with triangles? Well, let's say you had a triangle BCE, with side $b = 6$, side $c = 4$, and angle $E = 73°$. With the laws of sine and cosine, you can solve the triangle.

Which will help you more here, the law of sines or cosines? Probably the law of cosines, because you have two of the sides. You are missing side e, so set side e as the unknown.

$$e^2 = b^2 + c^2 - 2bc \ \cos E$$

Now you can put your information into the formula.

$$e^2 = 6^2 + 4^2 - 2(24)(.2924)$$
$$e^2 = 36 + 16 - (48)(.2924)$$
$$e^2 = 52 - 14.04$$
$e^2 = 37.96$, and $e = \sqrt{37.96}$, or approximately 6.16.

Now you have all three sides. To find angles B and C you can use the law of sines.

$$\dfrac{\sin C}{c} = \dfrac{\sin E}{e}$$

$\dfrac{\sin C}{4} = \dfrac{.9563}{6.16}$ (Note that the sine of 73° is used here, not the cosine.)

$\sin C = .621$, so $\angle C$ measures approximately 38°23'.

To find $\angle B$, add $\angle C$ and $\angle E$ and subtract from 180°.

$$B = 180° - (73° + 38°23') = 68°37'$$

And you've solved the triangle.
Try another to get yourself in the groove.

Example

Triangle ABC has side $a = 4$, and angles $B = 35°$ and $C = 75°$. Solve the triangle.

If you have two out of three angles in a triangle, it's pretty easy to find the third angle from the rule of 180. Here, the third angle, $\angle A$, must be 70°. What is the easiest, and therefore the best, law to use to find the other sides? The law of sines.

$$\frac{\sin A}{a} = \frac{\sin B}{b}$$

$$\frac{.9397}{4} = \frac{.5736}{b}$$

$$b = 2.44$$

Side c can be found the same way.

$$\frac{\sin A}{a} = \frac{\sin C}{c}$$

$$\frac{.9397}{4} = \frac{.9659}{c}$$

$$c = 4.11$$

EXERCISE 13.4

Solve the following triangles, rounding to two decimal places.

1. Triangle ABC has side $a = 42$, $\angle A = 52°$, $\angle B = 61°$.

2. Triangle ABC has side $a = 20$, $\angle B = 30°$, and $\angle C = 70°$.

3. Triangle ABC has sides $a = 50$, $b = 40$, and $\angle C = 65°$.

4. Triangle ABC has sides $a = 6$, $b = 4$, and $c = 5$.

5. Triangle ABC has sides $a = 6$, $b = 8$, and $c = 10$.

6. Triangle ABC has sides $a = 14$, $c = 12$, and $\angle C = 58°$.

7. Triangle ABC has sides $b = 10$, $c = 12$, and $\angle A = 47°$.

8. Triangle ABC has side $b = 100$, $\angle A = 85°$, and $\angle C = 50°$.

ANSWERS TO CHAPTER THIRTEEN EXERCISES

ANSWERS TO EXERCISE 13.1

1. $\cos B = \dfrac{a}{c}$; $\tan B = \dfrac{b}{a}$; $\csc B = \dfrac{c}{b}$; $\sec B = \dfrac{c}{a}$; $\cot B = \dfrac{a}{b}$

2. $\sin B = \dfrac{9}{\sqrt{130}}$ or $\dfrac{9\sqrt{130}}{130}$, $\tan B = \dfrac{9}{7}$; $\csc B = \dfrac{\sqrt{130}}{9}$;

   $\sec B = \dfrac{\sqrt{130}}{7}$; $\cot B = \dfrac{7}{9}$

3. $\dfrac{3}{5}$

4. $\sin A$

5. They are the same.

6. $\tan A$

7. $\cot B$

8. They are the same.

ANSWERS TO EXERCISE 13.2

1. 0.45

2. 0.45

3. 2.18

4. 1.41

5. 1.42

6. 2.75

7. 0.58

8. 0.58

ANSWERS TO EXERCISE 13.3

1. $\angle B = 62°$, $c = 15.85$, $a = 7.44$

2. $\angle A = 62°$, $a = 41.37$, $c = 46.86$

3. $\angle A = 39°$, $\angle B = 51°$, $a = 18.88$, $b = 23.31$

4. $\angle B = 40°$, $a = 20$, $\angle A = 50°$, $c = 26.11$, $b = 16.78$

5. $\angle B = 45°$, $\angle A = 45°$, $c = 70$, a and $b = 49.50$

6. The balloon is 47.67 feet above the dog.

7. 33.18 feet from the overpass. Remember, the angle of depression here is complementary to the top angle of the triangle.

8. The rope must be 97.08 feet long.

ANSWERS TO EXERCISE 13.4

1. $\angle C = 67°$, $b = 46.62$, $c = 49.06$

2. $\angle A = 80°$, $c = 19.08$, $b = 10.15$

3. $\angle A = 67°24'$, and $\angle B = 47°36'$, $c = 49.09$

4. $\angle A = 82°49'$, $\angle B = 41°25'$, $\angle C = 55°46'$

5. $\angle C = 90°$, $\angle B = 53°8'$, $\angle A = 36°52'$

6. $\angle C = 58°$, $\angle A = 81°39'$, $\angle B = 40°21'$, $b = 9.16$

7. $\angle C = 78°18'$, $\angle B = 54°42'$, $a = 8.962$

8. $c = 108.3$, $\angle B = 45°$, $a = 140.9$

Trigonometry of Radians

14

RADIANS AND THE UNIT CIRCLE

As you may have noticed, there are certain triangles and angles that the trigonometry we have looked at so far has not covered. For instance, what about obtuse triangles that contain angles over 90 degrees? To work with these angles we need to use trigonometry that is in a slightly different geometric realm; the realm of coordinate geometry. The sort of trigonometry you are about to learn is, in fact, the sort of trigonometry you'll see in most advanced math. How is it different from what we've experienced so far? In lots of ways. First of all, it uses different units.

The unit circle is the base of these units; the unit circle has the equation $x^2 + y^2 = 1$. It looks like this:

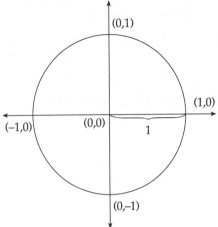

Its circumference is 2π (since its radius is 1), and this 2π is an important measure. Instead of degrees, the angle measures of a unit circle are expressed in **radians**. There are 2π radians in an entire circle, which is basically an angle of 360°. The radian measure of a straight line is π, and, as you know, a straight line is an angle of 180°. One radian is equal to approximately 57.3°; one degree is equal to .02 radians. How do you find the length of an arc opposite one of these radian-measured angles? Well, the length of an arc on the unit circle is the same measure, in radians, as the angle that the arc corresponds to. An arc corresponding to an *angle* of π radians has a *length* of π radians (also known as 180°).

For practice, convert the following degree measures into radians, or the reverse, as asked.

EXERCISE 14.1

1. How many radians is 270°?

2. How many radians is 90°?

3. How many radians is 60°?

4. How many radians is 30°?

5. How many degrees is 4π radians?

6. How many degrees is $\dfrac{\pi}{6}$ radian?

7. How many degrees is 7π radians?

8. How many degrees is $\dfrac{\pi}{5}$ radian?

THE ANGLES AND THEIR NAMES

The symbol used to represent angles in trigonometry is the Greek letter θ, pronounced **theta**. Essentially, θ represents an unknown angle measure, almost always expressed in radians. Any angle θ has two sides. Its **initial side**, which for angles in the **standard position**, is the positive part of the x-axis of the unit circle, and its **terminal side**. Angles with positive measures are thought of as beginning at the initial side and rotating counter-clockwise.

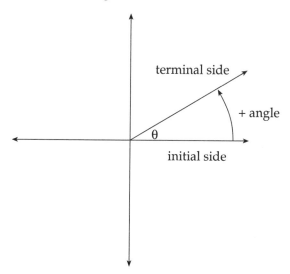

A negative angle moves clockwise from the initial side.

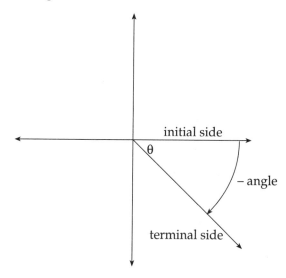

Angles in non-standard positions may have their initial sides elsewhere, but we won't concern ourselves with them for the moment.

The terminal side of an angle may extend more than 2π radians from the initial side, in either direction.

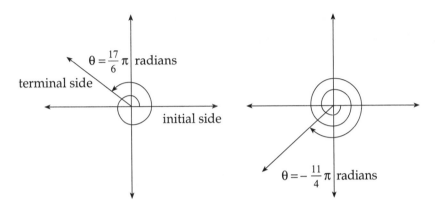

TRIGONOMETRIC FUNCTIONS OF ANGLES MEASURED IN RADIANS

The trigonometric functions of the angle θ are what all of the fuss is about, and here is where you can see the beauty of using the unit circle. The functions themselves remain the same—sine is opposite over hypotenuse, cosine is adjacent over hypotenuse, and so on. But in a unit circle, all of these sides have specific values.

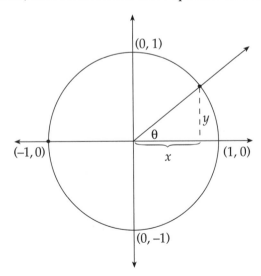

Since the hypotenuse is the radius of the unit circle, it is always 1. So the sine of θ is always $\frac{y}{1}$ or y, the cosine of θ is always $\frac{x}{1}$ or x, and the tangent of θ is $\frac{y}{x}$.

$$\sin\ θ = y \qquad\qquad \csc\ θ = \frac{1}{y}$$

$$\cos\ θ = x \qquad\qquad \sec\ θ = \frac{1}{x}$$

$$\tan\ θ = \frac{y}{x} \qquad\qquad \cot\ θ = \frac{y}{x}$$

Neat and lovely, you may be saying to yourself, but how does this get us any closer to finding the functions of non-acute angles? Before we reach that point, there are some more things that you must know. While the trigonometric functions are easy to find from the unit circle, the signs of their values change depending on which quadrant the terminal side of the angle falls. All of the trigonometric functions in the first quadrant are positive. From then on, the signs vary like so:

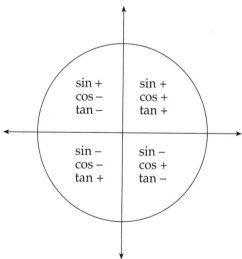

You will need to remember this. From this information we get closer to finding out about angles greater than $\frac{\pi}{2}$ radians, or 90 degrees. For angles between $\frac{\pi}{2}$ and π, the sine of θ is the sine of the closest acute angle formed by the x-axis and the terminal side. Some people call this smaller angle alpha, from the Greek letter α; it can also be called phi from the Greek letter ϕ. You can also look at it as θ', q, t, k or whatever your heart desires. Any way you name it, the trigonometric function of this acute angle, when given the appropriate sign for its quadrant, will give you the sine of θ for the original obtuse angle.

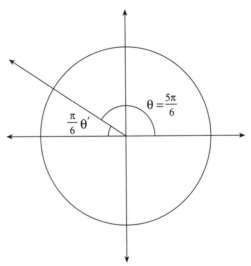

Thus, $\sin \theta = \sin \frac{5\pi}{6} = \sin \frac{\pi}{6}$; since the terminal side is in quadrant II, sine is positive, so this equals $\sin \frac{\pi}{6}$, which is $-\frac{1}{2}$.

THE BIG ANGLES IN TOWN

How do we know that $\sin \frac{\pi}{6}$ is $\frac{1}{2}$? Well, we could convert radians to degrees and see that we are looking at the sine of 30°, which we know is $\frac{1}{2}$ from our previous discussion regarding the special triangle functions (page 200 if your memory is a little hazy). We could also learn the function values of radian angles by looking at a table made up of trigonometric functions of radian angles, or by using the trig functions on a calculator set to the radian mode. If we had the (x, y) coordinates of the point at which the terminal side of the angle intercepted the unit circle we'd be in terrific shape, because we know that the sine is y. Any of these are fine methods, but just for good measure, we're going to outline the functions of those angles you are most likely to run across. You might want to sketch these in on a unit circle yourself to see the special right triangles they form. This will show you how these values were derived. Look at the values; think about them and how they relate to special right triangles and the unit circle, and you'll see how they make sense.

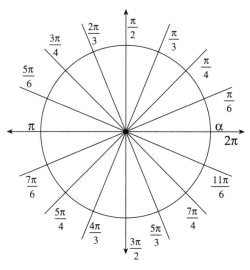

	0	$\dfrac{\pi}{6}$	$\dfrac{\pi}{4}$	$\dfrac{\pi}{3}$	$\dfrac{\pi}{2}$	π	2π
sin	0	$\dfrac{1}{2}$	$\dfrac{1}{2}\sqrt{2}$	$\dfrac{1}{2}\sqrt{3}$	1	0	0
cos	1	$\dfrac{1}{2}\sqrt{3}$	$\dfrac{1}{2}\sqrt{2}$	$\dfrac{1}{2}$	0	-1	1
tan	0	$\dfrac{\sqrt{3}}{3}$	1	$\sqrt{3}$	undefined	0	0

The other function values—the reciprocal functions—can be determined from these, and the function values of the obtuse and negative angles can also be determined from these.

Example

What is the cosine of an angle θ of $\dfrac{5\pi}{3}$ radians?

One of the easiest places to start is by drawing this angle in the unit circle to see which quadrant the terminal side falls in, and to see what angle you'll be finding the cosine of. You can do this by moving $\dfrac{\pi}{3}$ around the circle—remember, three of these will make an angle of π radians, or a straight line—until you get five of them.

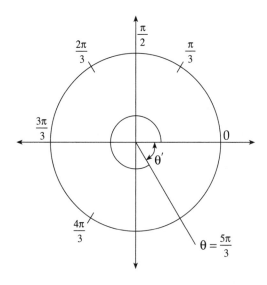

The terminal side falls in the fourth quadrant, so the cosine will be positive. And, since this is an obtuse angle, we know that we'll be looking for the cosine of the acute angle that the terminal side forms with the x-axis. The closest half of the x-axis is made by 2π, so subtract $\dfrac{5\pi}{3}$ from 2π to get the acute angle, $\dfrac{\pi}{3}$. The cosine of the angle θ is the cosine of the acute angle $\dfrac{\pi}{3}$, which is $\dfrac{1}{2}$. See how helpful it is to know those special angles?

IDENTITIES

Since trigonometry is based on ratios, all of the trigonometric functions have consistent relationships to one another. These relationships, and the truths about the various functions they express, are called **identities**.

The first set of relationships of this kind were set out on page 201. The next set will, as you can see, be extremely helpful within the province of trigonometry and the unit circle. They apply to negative angles—angles that are the result of the terminal side moving in a clockwise direction from the initial side.

$$\sin (-\theta) = -\sin \theta \qquad \csc (-\theta) = -\csc \theta$$

$$\cos (-\theta) = \cos \theta \qquad \sec (-\theta) = \sec \theta$$

$$\tan (-\theta) = -\tan \theta \qquad \cot (-\theta) = -\cot \theta$$

There are other identities that become necessary when trigonometric functions are being manipulated. Since the formula for the unit circle is $x^2 + y^2 = 1$, and $\sin \theta = y$, and $\cos \theta = x$, we can deduce that $(\sin \theta)^2 + (\cos \theta)^2 = 1$. It also helps to know, in this case, that $(\sin \theta)^2 = \sin^2 \theta$, and $(\cos \theta)^2 = \cos^2 \theta$. Officially, then, this is the way the identity looks: $\sin^2 \theta + \cos^2 \theta = 1$.

From this identity we can determine other identities. By dividing both sides by $\cos^2 \theta$, we end up with $\tan^2 \theta + 1 = \sec^2 \theta$.

Starting again with $\sin^2 \theta + \cos^2 \theta = 1$, but dividing this time by $\sin^2 \theta$, we get: $1 + \cot^2 \theta = \csc^2 \theta$. And these are some extremely useful identities.

$$\sin^2 \theta + \cos^2 \theta = 1$$

$$\tan^2 \theta + 1 = \sec^2 \theta$$

$$1 + \cot^2 \theta = \csc^2 \theta$$

GRAPHS OF THE FUNCTIONS

Trigonometric functions are functions, after all, which means that they can be graphed. Even more, these graphs are quite useful in real-life applications like harmonics, light, engineering, rotations, and all sorts of fascinating vibrations, most of which you'll see later in your mathematical career. The ways in which graphs of trig functions will be important right now, unfortunately, is as answers on trigonometry tests.

For now you will have to be satisfied with remembering the identifying marks of the various graphs, and noting the ways in which the graphs repeat themselves. We can demonstrate this most easily by looking at the graph of sin θ. Remember that handy chart that showed the sines of different values of θ? Here is what that would look like, graphed.

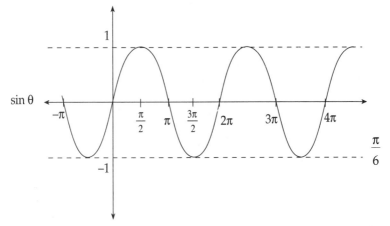

Does it remind you of anything? An EKG? The cover of Pink Floyd's *Dark Side of the Moon?* It might remind you of either of those things because they both represent **periodic graphs**. A periodic graph repeats itself at specific intervals. The graph of the function of sin θ is periodic with period 2π.

That means that at every 2π interval, the graph repeats itself. The function of cos θ can also be graphed.

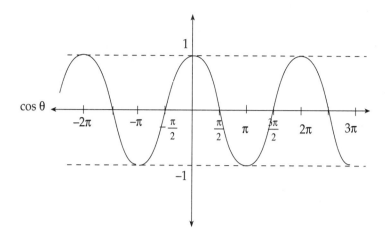

From the graph you can see that the function of $\cos\theta$ is also periodic with period 2π.

That leaves us to determine the graph of $\tan\theta$.

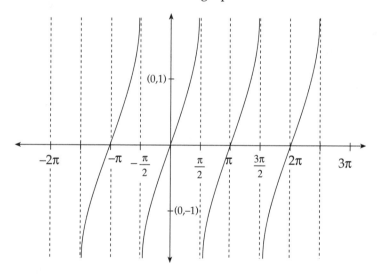

As you can see, this function is periodic not with period 2π but with period π. What else can we see from the tangent's graph? Well, it has vertical asymptotes at $x = \dfrac{\pi}{2}$, as well as at every line x a distance of π away from $\dfrac{\pi}{2}$.

INVERSE TRIGONOMETRIC FUNCTIONS AND MORE GRAPHS

You've probably already come across a question or two in which you had to determine the value of the angle from its sine, cosine, or some other function. And you probably wondered whether there was some function, or formula, or *something*, that you could use to get this. What you were instinctively feeling around for is what we call the **inverse trigonometric function**. It is denoted in a rather tricky way: If the known is sin x, the inverse function (the degree or radian measure of the corresponding angle) is either arcsin x or sin^{-1} x. Both of these mean exactly the same thing. Do not be fooled by the similarity of the floating negative to an exponent; it is definitely not an exponent. It is simply one of the ways (perhaps the not-so-very-intelligent way) that an inverse function is expressed. The ways these two are pronounced are "the arc sine of x" or "the inverse sine of x."

There are some limitations to the inverse trigonometric functions. A question might ask: *What is arcsin 1?* And, as you may have noticed, there are a whole lot of angles that could have a sine of 1. This presents one problem. The other problem becomes clear when you try to graph this function. The following represents a graph of $y = \sin^{-1} x$.

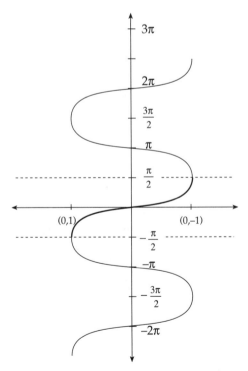

As you can see, this graph doesn't at present represent the graph of a function at all. A function can have only one value of y for each value of x; this graph fails the vertical line test (page 142). So what did mathematicians do about this? They decided that the range of values for the inverse function must be restricted for two reasons: To provide these problems with unique solutions, and to make this graph represent an actual function, in which for every value of x there is one, and only one, value of y. To effect this, mathematicians said that for $y = \sin^{-1} x$, it must be true that $x = \sin y$, which means that $-\frac{\pi}{2} \le x \le \frac{\pi}{2}$. This is represented by the darkened portion of the graph, which, as you can see, represents a function.

This same state of affairs exists for the other inverse functions, and the situations are dealt with in the same way. Thus, $\cos^{-1} x = y$ (or $y = \arccos x$) is only a function if $0 \le x \le \pi$, and $\tan^{-1} x = y$ (or $\arctan x = y$ if you'd rather), x must be between $-\frac{\pi}{2}$ and $\frac{\pi}{2}$, but cannot be equal to either due to the vertical asymptotes.

Example

What is arctan 1?

Since arctan is an inverse function, you know that you're looking for an angle that has a tangent of 1. Either you can look at your tables, or you can hearken back in your memory and try to think of those common trigonometric values you saw earlier. What is tangent, again? It's x over y, or sine over cosine. When are sine and cosine equal, giving 1 for a tangent? When you have an isosceles right triangle, which means that the angle is $\frac{\pi}{4}$ radians. This angle falls within the acceptable values for the inverse functions, so you're in business. So the arctan of 1 is $\frac{\pi}{4}$.

Try some on your own to get the hang of it.

EXERCISE 14.2

1. What is arcsin 1?

2. What is $\sin^{-1} \frac{1}{2}$?

3. What is $\tan^{-1} \sqrt{3}$?

4. What is $\arccos \frac{\sqrt{2}}{2}$?

5. What is $\tan^{-1} \frac{\sqrt{3}}{3}$?

6. What is $\cos\left(\sin^{-1}\dfrac{\sqrt{3}}{2}\right)$?

7. What is $\tan\left(\tan^{-1}\sqrt{3}\right)$?

8. What is $\sin\left(\tan^{-1}\dfrac{\sqrt{3}}{3}\right)$?

ONE MORE BATCH OF IDENTITIES

What happens when trigonometric functions are combined? Of course it isn't as beautifully simple as just adding, multiplying, or subtracting the functions. The addition (and subtraction, and a whole lot else) of trigonometric functions follow laws.

The **addition laws**: For any two angles θ and ϕ, their functions are combined as follows.

$\sin(\theta + \phi) = \sin\theta\cos\phi + \cos\theta\sin\phi$

$\cos(\theta + \phi) = \cos\theta\cos\phi - \sin\theta\sin\phi$

$\tan(\theta + \phi) = \dfrac{\tan\theta + \tan\phi}{1 - \tan\theta\tan\phi}$

How do you know that you can't just add the two sines of the angles? Wouldn't that be easier? Well, sure it would be easier, but it would also be wrong. Take a look at what would happen if we worked it out with angles that we actually know.

If the angles were $\dfrac{\pi}{2}$ and $\dfrac{\pi}{4}$, we can find that

$\sin\left(\dfrac{\pi}{2} + \dfrac{\pi}{4}\right) = \sin\dfrac{3\pi}{4} = \dfrac{\sqrt{2}}{2}$

But, if you were just to take the sine of each and add them, you would get $\sin\dfrac{\pi}{2} + \sin\dfrac{\pi}{4} = 1 + \dfrac{\sqrt{2}}{2} = \dfrac{2+\sqrt{2}}{2}$; a very different value.

The **subtraction laws** are as follows:

$\sin(\theta - \phi) = \sin\theta\cos - \cos\theta\sin$

$\cos(\theta - \phi) = \cos\cos - \sin\sin$

$\tan(\theta - \phi) = \dfrac{\tan\theta - \tan\phi}{1 + \tan\theta\tan\phi}$

How does one prove these, or any, identities? These identities will be proved in the upcoming paragraphs.

It will fall to you to prove other identities, however. Proving an identity is a lot like trying to find the right outfit to wear; it's all daring and experimentation. Where do you start? Well, usually one side of an identity will be uglier or more complicated. To prove the identity, approach this nasty side and try to rewrite it, using the identities you already know. For instance, if you see $\cos^2\theta$, you might rewrite it as $1 - \sin^2\theta$ (page 215). All of the basic identities are in the appendix, and you should refer to this list when you begin to prove identities on your own (we've included a few questions at the end of this chapter). Rewrite and rewrite until the side that was originally ugly is transformed into the other side. Proving identities is a lot of trial and error. If one side isn't working, try the other side. What you want to do is show that they equal one another.

You'll get more practiced at it the more you do it, of course, and the most important bit of advice that we can give you is this: The point is the *process*, not getting the right answer. The point of figuring out identities is to improve your math skills, not to reach the end point of identities themselves.

At any rate, the way in which the subtraction identity for cosines is proved is by the distance formula. Take a look at a unit circle with two angles θ and ϕ.

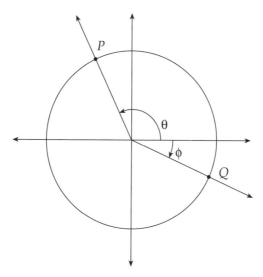

Notice that ϕ is a negative angle (crafty, aren't we?) and θ is a positive angle. The point P is where the terminal side of the angle θ intersects the unit circle; it has coordinates $(x\theta, y\theta)$, also known in trig terminology as $(\cos\theta, \sin\theta)$. The point Q is where the terminal side of the angle ϕ intersects the unit circle, and it has coordinates $(x\phi, y\phi)$, or $(\cos\phi, \sin\phi)$. Okay so far? If not, read through this paragraph again. Now, the distance formula (page 139) can give us the direct distance between P and Q. To make things easier, we'll find the squared distance (to get rid of irritating negatives); we designate this distance PQ^2.

$$PQ^2 = (\cos\theta - \cos\phi)^2 + (\sin\theta - \sin\phi)^2$$
$$PQ^2 = (\cos^2\theta - 2\cos\theta\cos\phi + \cos^2\phi) + (\sin^2\theta - 2\sin\theta\sin\phi + \sin^2\phi)$$

Combining them, you can use that wonderful identity you learned previously, $\sin^2\theta + \cos^2\theta = 1$. It will work for any angle, so we reorganize and then simplify.

$$PQ^2 = (\cos^2\theta + \sin^2\theta) + (\cos^2\phi + \sin^2\phi) - 2(\cos\theta\cos\phi + \sin\theta\sin\phi)$$
$$PQ^2 = 1 + 1 - 2(\cos\theta\cos\phi + \sin\theta\sin\phi)$$
$$PQ^2 = 2 - 2(\cos\theta\cos\phi + \sin\theta\sin\phi)$$

That in itself might not get you very far, but don't worry, there's more. You can shift those angles around the circle by subtracting the angle ϕ from each angle, creating new angles $\theta - \phi$ and $\phi - \phi$. Since the angle ϕ is negative, the angles move counter-clockwise to the positive side, because you're subtracting a negative.

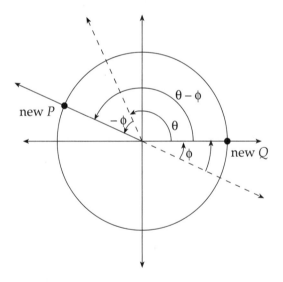

The new terminal sides are marked here, with their new end points, and as you can see from the diagrams, the new P (or P') and the new Q (or Q') will have the same distance between them because that distance is opposite the same angle, just shifted counter-clockwise a distance of ϕ. Use the distance formula again with $P'Q'$, but now the coordinates of P' are $(\cos\theta - \phi, \sin\theta - \phi)$. The coordinates for Q'? Well, they are $(\cos \phi - \phi, \sin \phi - \phi)$, which fall on your unit circle at $(1, 0)$. How convenient.

$$P'Q'^2 = (\cos (\theta - \phi) - 1)^2 + (\sin (\theta - \phi) - 0)^2$$
$$P'Q'^2 = \cos^2(\theta - \phi) - 2\cos (\theta - \phi) + 1 + \sin^2 (\theta - \phi).$$

Again we can use the information that $\sin^2 \theta + \cos^2 \theta = 1$. Regroup.
$$P'Q'^2 = [\cos^2(\theta - \phi) + \sin^2 (\theta - \phi)] + 1 - 2\cos (\theta - \phi)$$
$$P'Q'^2 = 1 + 1 - 2\cos (\theta - \phi) = 2 - 2\cos (\theta - \phi)$$

The beauty of the situation becomes apparent: $P'Q'$ is equal to PQ, so:

$$2 - 2\cos (\theta - \phi) = 2 - 2(\cos \theta \cos \phi + \sin \theta \sin \phi).$$

Subtract 2 from both sides, and then divide both sides by -2:

$$\cos (\theta - \phi) = \cos \theta \cos \phi + \sin \theta \sin \phi$$

Funny, doesn't that look a whole lot like the law of subtraction for cosines? Well, that's how it works.

To prove the identity for the addition law for cosines you can switch your negative angle ϕ for $-\phi$, put it into your subtraction law, and see that subtracting a negative gives you addition.

$$\cos (\theta - (-\phi)) = \cos \theta \cos (-\phi) + \sin \theta \sin (-\phi)$$

Remember that $\sin -\theta = -\sin \theta$, and $\cos -\theta = \cos \theta$, and simplify.

$$\cos (\theta + \phi) = \cos \theta \cos \phi - \sin \theta \sin \phi$$

And that's the addition law for cosines.

To establish the addition law for sines you first go back in time, to when you first started reading trig tables. You realized then that they only go up to 45 degrees—or $\frac{\pi}{2}$—because the sine of an angle, or $\sin \theta$ as you can say it now, is equal to the cosine of 90 degrees minus that angle, or $\frac{\pi}{2} - \theta$. This is true, of course, in the other direction as well. The cosine of an angle is equal to the sine of 90 degrees minus that angle, or $\frac{\pi}{2} - \theta$. Take a minute to go back to page 194 to refresh your memory on this if you have any trouble with it.

You can then figure out from this (and a bit more), how to find the sine of added angles.

$$\sin (\theta + \phi) = \cos \left[\frac{\pi}{2} - (\theta + \phi) \right]$$

For clarity, rearrange.

$$\sin (\theta + \phi) = \cos \left[\left(\frac{\pi}{2} - \theta \right) - \phi \right]$$

Now you can use the subtraction law of cosines that you worked so hard to establish.

$$\sin (\theta + \phi) = \cos \left(\frac{\pi}{2} - \theta \right) \cos \phi + \sin \left(\frac{\pi}{2} - \theta \right) \sin \phi$$

Since you just happen to know that the cosine of $\frac{\pi}{2} - \theta$ is equal to the sine of θ, and the sine of $\frac{\pi}{2} - \theta$ is equal to the cosine of θ, you can rewrite this:

$$\sin (\theta + \phi) = \sin \theta \cos \phi + \cos \theta \sin \phi$$

And that's the addition law for sines. If, as you did earlier with the law for cosines, you used $- \phi$ instead, you would come up with the subtraction law for sines.

TANGENTS, THEIR LAWS, AND THEIR SOCIETY

How can you show the addition and subtraction laws for tangents? They follow from the laws for sines and cosines.

First, show that tangent is, as always, sine over cosine.

$$\tan (\theta + \phi) = \frac{\sin (\theta + \phi)}{\cos (\theta + \phi)}$$

Now you can take advantage of the addition laws for cosines and sines.

$$\tan (\theta + \phi) = \frac{\sin \theta \cos \phi + \cos \theta \sin \phi}{\cos \theta \cos \phi - \sin \theta \sin \phi}$$

The fraction can be simplified by dividing both the top and the bottom by $\cos \theta \cos \phi$. As you well know, dividing (or multiplying, for that matter) both the top and bottom of a fraction by any nonzero number doesn't change the overall value of the fraction.

$$\tan (\theta + \phi) = \frac{\dfrac{\sin \theta \cos \phi}{\cos \theta \cos \phi} + \dfrac{\cos \theta \sin \phi}{\cos \theta \cos \phi}}{\dfrac{\cos \theta \cos \phi}{\cos \theta \cos \phi} - \dfrac{\sin \theta \sin \phi}{\cos \theta \cos \phi}}$$

$$\tan(\theta + \phi) = \frac{\dfrac{\sin\theta}{\cos\theta} + \dfrac{\sin\phi}{\cos\phi}}{1 - \left(\dfrac{\sin\theta}{\cos\theta}\right)\left(\dfrac{\sin\phi}{\cos\phi}\right)}$$

You've proven the identity; since sine over cosine is tangent, all you have to do is rewrite it.

$$\tan(\theta + \phi) = \frac{\tan\theta + \tan\phi}{1 - \tan\theta\tan\phi}$$

MORE IDENTITIES?!?

There are two other main identities that you must know, and they follow from the identities you are already familiar with; the laws of addition and subtraction.

The two new ones are the **double-angle formulas** and the **half-angle formulas**. How do they work? First, the double-angle formula. We can show that it's an identity by using $(\theta + \theta)$ instead of $(\theta + \phi)$ in the addition law for sines and cosines, thereby creating a double angle.

$$\sin(\theta + \theta) = \sin\theta\cos\theta + \cos\theta\sin\theta$$

The formula, when it's cleaned up, looks like this.

$$\sin 2\theta = 2\sin\theta\cos\theta$$

The double-angle formula for cosines is derived in the same way.

$$\cos(\theta + \theta) = \cos\theta\cos\theta - \sin\theta\sin\theta$$

The double-angle formula for cosines looks like this.

$$\cos 2\theta = \cos^2\theta - \sin^2\theta$$

And the double angle formula for tangents, though not nearly as useful as the other two, is found in the same way. It ends up looking like this.

$$\tan 2\theta = \frac{2\tan\theta}{1 - \tan^2\theta}$$

HALF–ANGLE FORMULAS

Half–angle formulas are somewhat different. We can establish the half–angle law for cosines by first looking at the double-angle formula, and then remembering an identity you learned a few pages back, $\sin^2\theta + \cos^2\theta = 1$, which we can rewrite as $\sin^2\theta = 1 - \cos^2\theta$. We can put this identity into the double-angle law of cosines.

$\cos 2\theta = \cos^2\theta - \sin^2\theta$

$\sin^2\theta$ is replaced by $1 - \cos^2\theta$

$\cos 2\theta = \cos^2\theta - (1 - \cos 2\theta)$

$\cos 2\theta = 2\cos^2\theta - 1$

To find the formula for half angles, we simply replace θ here with $\frac{1}{2}\theta$.

$$\cos 2\left(\frac{\theta}{2}\right) = 2\cos^2\left(\frac{\theta}{2}\right) - 1$$

Cancel the 2's on the left side.

$$\cos\theta = 2\cos^2\left(\frac{\theta}{2}\right) - 1$$

Now you can solve for $\cos\frac{\theta}{2}$.

$$\cos\theta + 1 = 2\cos^2\left(\frac{\theta}{2}\right)$$

$$\frac{1 + \cos\theta}{2} = \cos^2\left(\frac{\theta}{2}\right)$$

$$\pm\sqrt{\frac{1 + \cos\theta}{2}} = \cos\frac{\theta}{2}$$

And that's the cosine of a half-angle. The sine for a half-angle is found in the same way. Often, though, the formulas are shown in the less-reduced fashion. Either way, of course, they say the same things. How about the half-angle formula for tangent? That's found the same way, too, but you don't have to worry about squaring it.

Here are the half-angle formulas.

$$2\cos^2\theta = 1 + \cos 2\theta$$

$$2\sin^2\theta = 1 - \cos 2\theta$$

$$\tan\theta = \frac{1 - \cos 2\theta}{\sin 2\theta}$$

These are the identities you must know if you are ever to feel truly comfortable in the realm of trigonometry and beyond. While it is true that you should know them by heart, probably your best course is not to memorize them in the accepted sense (staying up all night so you can correctly pronounce them without really knowing what you are saying). Try using a piece of paper on which all of the identities are written out as you work through some identity questions; feel free to refer to this paper. The more you use the identities the more you will understand them, and the easier it will be to write them from memory.

How are they going to be used? You'll probably be asked to prove identities in much the same way we did here, by using other identities.

Example

Show that $(\tan\theta + \cot\theta)(\cos\theta + \sin\theta) = \sec\theta + \csc\theta$ is an identity.

The easiest first step is to make one side simpler, so you can take the more complex side and show it to be equal to the simple side. Here, the second expression on the left is simple, so to get rid of the far left-hand expression we can divide both sides by that far left-hand piece, $(\tan\theta + \cot\theta)$.

$$\cos\theta + \sin\theta = \frac{\sec\theta + \csc\theta}{\tan\theta + \cot\theta}$$

Now you can try to make the right side into the left side. First, show the functions in the form of cosines and sines by remembering their identities: tangent is sine over cosine, cotangent is cosine over sine, secant is one over cosine, cosecant is one over sine.

$$\frac{\sec\theta + \csc\theta}{\tan\theta + \cot\theta} \text{ becomes } \frac{\dfrac{1}{\cos\theta} + \dfrac{1}{\sin\theta}}{\dfrac{\sin\theta}{\cos\theta} + \dfrac{\cos\theta}{\sin\theta}}$$

Fully add the top and the bottom of the fraction to make life easier.

$$\frac{\dfrac{\sin\theta + \cos\theta}{\cos\theta\sin\theta}}{\dfrac{\sin^2\theta + \cos^2\theta}{\cos\theta\sin\theta}}$$

Now there are more identities you can use. What is $\sin^2\theta + \cos^2\theta$ again? Why, it's 1. You can rewrite the fraction, and then divide.

$$\dfrac{\dfrac{\sin\theta + \cos\theta}{\cos\theta\sin\theta}}{\dfrac{1}{\cos\theta\sin\theta}} \text{ becomes } \left(\dfrac{\sin\theta + \cos\theta}{\cos\theta\sin\theta}\right)\cdot\left(\dfrac{\cos\theta\,\cos\theta}{1}\right) = \sin\theta + \cos\theta,$$

which is the other side. You've got yourself another identity.

EXERCISE 14.3

1. Rewrite $\cos^2\theta$ entirely in terms of $\sin\theta$.

2. Rewrite $\sec^2\theta$ entirely in terms of $\sin\theta$.

3. Rewrite $\tan^2\theta$ entirely in terms of $\cos\theta$.

4. Rewrite $\cot^2\theta$ entirely in terms of $\tan\theta$.

5. Rewrite $\tan^2\theta$ entirely in terms of $\sec\theta$.

6. Show that $\csc\theta - \sin\theta = \cot\theta\,\cos\theta$.

7. Show that $\cos\theta\,\sec\theta = 1$.

8. Show that $\dfrac{\sin\theta + \tan\theta}{\csc\theta + \cot\theta} = \sin\theta\tan\theta$

ANSWERS TO CHAPTER FOURTEEN EXERCISES

ANSWERS TO EXERCISE 14.1

1. $\dfrac{3\pi}{2}$

2. $\dfrac{\pi}{2}$

3. $\dfrac{\pi}{3}$

4. $\dfrac{\pi}{6}$

5. $720°$

6. $30°$

7. $1260°$

8. $36°$

ANSWERS TO EXERCISE 14.2

1. $\dfrac{\pi}{2}$

2. $\dfrac{\pi}{6}$

3. $\dfrac{\pi}{3}$

4. $\dfrac{\pi}{4}$

5. $\dfrac{\pi}{6}$

6. $\dfrac{1}{2}$

7. $\sqrt{3}$

8. $\dfrac{1}{2}$

ANSWERS TO EXERCISE 14.3

1. $1 - \sin^2 \theta$

2. $\dfrac{1}{1 - \sin^2 \theta}$

3. $\dfrac{1}{\cos^2 \theta} - 1$

4. $\dfrac{1}{\tan^2 \theta}$

5. $\sec^2 \theta - 1$

6. Here's one way to do it. Start with the left side and change the csc into $\dfrac{1}{\sin \theta}$, then subtract $\sin \theta$ from that using the bow tie. You get $\dfrac{1 - \sin^2 \theta}{\sin \theta}$. The numerator of the fraction can be seen as $\cos^2 \theta$, so you have $\dfrac{\cos \theta \cos \theta}{\sin \theta}$, which can also be $\cot \theta \cos \theta$. And you've done it.

7. Here you can start with the left side, and change $\sec\theta$ into $\dfrac{1}{\cos\theta}$. You then get cosine over cosine, which of course equals 1.

8. Start with the left side one more time (if you like). Change the tangent, the cosecant and the cotangent into their related functions: $\dfrac{\sin\theta + \dfrac{\sin\theta}{\cos\theta}}{\dfrac{1}{\sin\theta} + \dfrac{\cos\theta}{\sin\theta}}$. Now simplify the numerator and denominator by finding common denominators if necessary, and adding them through.

You get $\dfrac{\dfrac{\sin\theta\cos\theta + \sin\theta}{\cos\theta}}{\dfrac{1 + \cos\theta}{\sin\theta}}$. Now factor the numerator of the top fraction to get $\sin\theta\,(\cos\theta + 1)$, and divide the top fraction by the bottom fraction by inverting the bottom and multiplying. You can cancel a lot, and you end up with $\dfrac{\sin^2\theta}{\cos\theta}$, which you can refigure as $\sin\theta$ over $\cos\theta$—also known as $\tan\theta$—times $\sin\theta$. You've proved the identity.

SO, HERE YOU ARE...

Well, you've worked your way through the whole book (we hope) and by now you have a firm grasp on the basics of algebra, geometry, and trigonometry. If this is as much math as you ever intend to cover, we hope you enjoyed it. But remember, what you've learned thus far leaves you on the very threshold of really terrific, interesting math, including calculus and beyond. So, if you're going further, enjoy the ride—it can be a great one.

Glossary

Absolute value or |x|: The distance on the number line between a number and 0, and that distance is always positive.

Acute angle: An angle that measures less than 90 degrees.

Algebraic expression: Algebraic terms combined by addition or subtraction.

Algebraic term: A variable, number, or a variable and a number combined by either multiplication or division.

Alternate interior angles: Angles formed by two parallel lines intersected by a third line; the ones that are between the two parallel lines, on opposite sides of the intersecting line, are alternate interior angles.

Angle of depression: The angle made from a viewer's eye to an object below the viewer.

Angle of elevation: The angle made from a viewer's eye to an object above the viewer.

Angles: The shapes formed when lines intersect.

Arcs: Sections of a circle's circumference.

Area: The number of square units a two-dimensional shape occupies.

Associative law: A law stating that no matter which way an operation of addition or multiplication is grouped, its result remains the same. $a \times (b \times c) = (a \times b) \times c$ and $(a + b) + c = a + (b + c)$

Asymptotes: The points at which a graphed line approaches infinity.

Axes: Plural of axis, usually refers to the x- and y-axes.

Axis (of a parabola): The line that intersects the parabola at the vertex and goes through the focus perpendicular to the directrix.

Base (of an exponent): The number that is being raised to an exponent.

Base (of a logarithm): The number in a logarithm that is raised to a power.

Base (of a shape): The bottom side or edge of a shape.

Binomial: An algebraic expression of two terms.

Binomial coefficients: $\binom{n}{n-1}$, also known as combinations, these give the coefficients for expansions of binomials raised to exponential powers.

Binomial theorem: A formula for the expansion of binomials raised to exponential powers.

$$(x+y)^n = \binom{n}{0} x^n y^0 + \binom{n}{1} x^{n-1}y^1 + \binom{n}{2} x^{n-2}y^2 + \binom{n}{n-1} x^{n-1}y^1 + \binom{n}{n} x^0 y^n$$

Brackets {}; **braces** or **fences** []: Variations of parentheses; used in this order: {[()]}.

Cartesian grid: The intersection of the x- and y-axes, used to locate points and lines.

Center: The point in the middle of a circle.

Chord: A line from one edge of the circle to another that does not go through the circle's center.

Circle: A round figure in which all points on the outside perimeter are equidistant from the point in the center.

Circumference: The measurement around the edge of a circle.

Coefficient: The number by which a variable is multiplied.

Combinations: The ways in which a number of objects can be selected from a larger group.

Commutative law: A law stating that any single operation of addition or multiplication is the same no matter what its order is. $a \times b = b \times a$ and $a + b = b + a$

Complementary angles: Two angles that add up to form a perpendicular, or 90°.

Completing the square: A way of solving trinomials by adding a missing third term that is half of the coefficient of x, squared.

Complex numbers: Numbers in which an imaginary number is combined with real numbers.

Cone: A rounded three-dimensional shape that tapers to a point.

Congruent: Having the same measure; equal.

Conic sections or **conics**: Shapes taken from different cross sections of a cone whose points maintain fixed ratios from a fixed point or points called the focus or foci, and (sometimes) a fixed external line which is called the directrix.

Constant: A term with a fixed numerical value within an expression or series of expressions.

Coordinate pair: A point on the coordinate plane that is identified by two coordinates.

Coordinate plane: The plane formed by the intersection of the x- and y-axes, used to locate points and lines.

Corresponding angle: The new, larger angle formed when the lines drawn from the ends of an inscribed angle meet at the circle's center.

cosecant or **csc**: The trigonometric function $\dfrac{hyp}{opp}$.

cosine or **cos**: The trigonometric function $\dfrac{adj}{hyp}$.

cotangent or **cot**: The trigonometric function $\dfrac{adj}{opp}$.

Cube: A three-dimensional shape of 6 square faces of equal dimensions.

Cylinder: A solid, tubular shape with two circular ends.

Degree (in plane geometry) or °: The standard measure of angles and lines in plane geometry. There are 180° in a line.

Degree (of a polynomial): A description of a polynomial that refers to the exponent involved.

Dependent variable: The value in a function that is the result of the other variable; its value is dependent on the value of the other. It is usually represented by y.

Diameter: Any line that passes from one side of the circle to the other through the center.

Directrix: The line that is at the same distance from a parabola as the parabola's focus.

Distance formula: $\sqrt{(x_2 - x_1)^2 + (y_2 - y_1)^2}$ represents the distance between two points, x_1, y_1 and x_2, y_2.

Distributive law: A law stating that multiplying by a combined sum is the same as multiplying by each part of the sum and then adding those multiplied parts. $a(b + c) = (ab) + (ac)$ and $a(b - c) = (ab) - (ac)$

Domain: The set of possible values for the independent variable of a particular function.

Eccentricity or e: The thinness of a shape; $e = \dfrac{c}{a}$ for an ellipse or a hyperbola.

Ellipse: A type of conic that looks something like a squashed circle. It maintains the same sum of the distances between any point on it and its two foci.

Equilateral triangle: A triangle with three equal sides and three equal angles.

Evaluating a formula: Solving a formula by putting in specific values.

Exponent: The small, superscript number that indicates how many of the base numbers are multiplied by each other.

Exterior angle: An angle on the outside of but adjacent to a shape.

Face: The flat surface of a three-dimensional shape.

Factorial or ! : The product of a number multiplied by each value of itself minus 1, then minus 2, then minus 3, decreasing until it reaches 1. $n! = n(n - 1)(n - 2)(n - 3) \ldots 1$

Focus or **foci**: The point or points used to define conic sections.

FOIL: The acronym for the order in which binomials are multiplied, First, Outside, Inside, Last.

Formulas: Algebraic equations that express fixed relationships.

Function: An expression of one variable's dependency on another.

Graph: The graphical or drawn expression of an equation.

Height: The measure from the top of a shape to its base via a perpendicular line.

Horizontal asymptote: The horizontal line set equal to y at which x approaches infinity, positive or negative.

Hyperbolas: Conics in which the *difference* of the distances between every point on their two foci is the same.

Hypotenuse: The side opposite the right angle in a right triangle.

Identities: Relationships, generally between trigonometric functions here, that always hold true.

Imaginary number or *i*: The square root of -1.

Independent variable: The value in a function that determines the value of the other variable. Its value is assigned without reference to the value of the other variable. It is usually represented by x.

Index: The small, superscript number next to the radical sign indicating the level of root (cube root, square root, fourth root, and so on).

Initial side: The side at which an angle begins on the unit circle; the positive side of the x-axis.

Integer: Any number that is not a decimal, fraction, or radical.

Interpolation: The process of finding a particular measurement by looking at the measurement of the surrounding values.

Inscribing: Putting a shape inside another shape so the vertices and ends of the non-circular shape touch the inside edge of the other shape.

Interior angle: An angle inside a shape.

Inverse trigonometric function: Shown as both arcsin x or $\sin^{-1} x$ (for sin; it works for all functions), this is a way of setting a trigonometric function equal to an angle measure.

Isosceles triangle: A triangle of two equal angles and two equal sides.

Lateral area: The area of a three-dimensional shape's side surface, excluding its top and base.

Law of cosines: For any triangle ABC, $c^2 = a^2 + b^2 - 2ab \cos C$, $a^2 = b^2 + c^2 - 2bc \cos A$, and $b^2 = a^2 + c^2 - 2ac \cos B$.

Law of sines: The law that states that for any triangle, the ratio of its angles' sines to their opposite sides is always equal. Triangle ABC $\dfrac{\sin A}{a} = \dfrac{\sin B}{b} = \dfrac{\sin C}{c}$.

Legs: The sides of a right triangle that are not the hypotenuse.

Line: An infinite number of points stretching along one dimension in both directions.

Linear polynomials: Polynomials of degree 1, mostly in the form of $ax + b$, where $a \neq 0$.

Line segments: Portions of lines.

Locus: The graphical or drawn expression of an equation or point.

Logarithm: An expression of an exponential power set to be solved for the exponent.

Major axis: A line through the foci of an ellipse the long way.

Minor arcs: Arcs of less than 180°.

Minor axis: A line through the center of an ellipse and perpendicular to the major axis.

Minutes: A unit of measurement of angles. Each geometric "degree" is made up of 60 minutes.

Monomial: An algebraic expression of one term.

Obtuse angle: An angle greater than 90°.

Order of operations: The order in which arithmetic operations are performed within an expression: Parentheses-Exponents-Multiplication-Division-Addition-Subtraction.

Origin: The place where the x- and y-axes meet (at the 0 point on both of them).

Parabola: A conic section that forms a curved line, and has all points equidistant from a point that is the focus, and a line that is the directrix.

Parallel lines | |: Lines that never meet and infinitely maintain the same distance between them.

Parentheses: A punctuation mark () used to group parts of expressions and make the orders of various mathematical operations clear.

Perimeter: The length around the edge of a two-dimensional shape.

Periodic graphs: A graph that repeats itself at specific intervals.

Periodic with period x: A way to note the specific intervals at which a periodic graph repeats itself. This particular one says that the graph repeats itself at every x interval.

Permutation: An expression of different possible arrangements.

Pi or **π**: the ratio of a circle's circumference to its diameter; also 3.1415927...or $\frac{22}{7}$.

Plane: A two-dimensional space extending infinitely in all directions.

Plane geometry: The geometry of flat or two-dimensional figures.

Point: A particular location in space without any depth, length, or width.

Point circle: A circle of radius 0.

Polynomial: An algebraic expression of one or more terms.

Power: The entire base number being raised to an exponent and the exponent, together.

Principle of mathematical induction: The principle that in order to prove that something is true for all positive integers n, you must prove that it is true for $n = 1$; in addition, you must prove that if it is true for $n = k$, it is also true for $n = k + 1$.

Pythagorean Theorem: The relationship between the length of the legs and the length of the hypotenuse of a right triangle as follows: $a^2 + b^2 = c^2$ in which c is the hypotenuse and a and b are the other legs of the right triangle.

Quadrants: The four main sections of the coordinate plane.

Quadratic formula: A formula that states that for $ax^2 + bx + c = 0$, where a is a nonzero number, $\dfrac{-b \pm \sqrt{b^2 - 4ac}}{2a}$ = the roots of the equation.

Quadratic polynomials: Polynomials of degree 2, usually in the form $ax^2 + bx + c$, where $a \neq 0$.

Quadrilateral: A closed two-dimensional shape that has four sides.

Radians: A unit of measurement based on the unit circle. A unit circle has a radius of 2π radians; π radians = $180°$.

Radical function: A function that contains a radical sign.

Radical sign $\sqrt{}$: A sign showing that a root is asked for; if there is no index, a square root is asked for.

Radius: A line that extends from the center of a circle to an edge.

Range: The set of all possible values for the dependent variable as well as the corresponding values for the independent variable of a function.

Rational function: A function that is the result of divided polynomials.

Rationalizing: Manipulating and removing the radical sign from some part of some number.

Real numbers: All positive and negative integers, fractions (regular and decimal fractions), and roots.

Rectangular prism: A three-dimensional solid, rectangular shape.

Right triangle: A triangle that contains a right angle.

Root (of exponents): A number which, when multiplied by itself, produces the number in question.

Roots (of quadratic equations): Solution(s) to a quadratic equation set equal to 0.

secant or **sec**: The trigonometric function $\frac{hyp}{adj}$.

Sector: The surface measure of an arc.

Similar triangles: Any two (or more) triangles whose corresponding angles are exactly equal.

Sine or **sin**: The trigonometric function $\frac{opposite}{hypotenuse}$.

Slant height: The height of a cone measured from the vertex to an edge of the base circle.

Slope: The measure of the steepness of a line.

Sphere: A three-dimensional, perfectly round shape.

Standard position: The position on the unit circle that most angles are drawn from, with one side on the x-axis and the vertex at the origin.

Supplementary angles: Two angles that together add up to the measure of a line, or 180°.

Surface area: The entire exterior surface of a three-dimensional object.

tangent or **tan**: The trigonometric function $\frac{opp}{adj}$.

Tangent (for a circle): Touching at one point, usually for a line touching the edge of a circle.

Terminal side: The side of an angle on the unit circle that moves away from the initial side.

Trigonometry: The branch of mathematics concerned with the measuring of triangles.

Trinomial: An algebraic expression of three terms.

Unit circle: A circle with its center at the origin of the coordinate plane, with a radius of one. It has equation $x^2 + y^2 = 1$.

Unknowns: The unknown value within an equation or expression; the value to be solved for.

Variable: A letter that stands in place of a number.

Vertex (of a conic): The point of a conic's most extreme curve, at which it begins to turn in the other direction.

Vertical angles: Equal angles that are opposite one another, formed by intersecting lines.

Vertical asymptote: The vertical line set equal to x at which y approaches infinity, positive or negative.

Vertical line test: A method for determining whether a graph represents a function by scanning it with a vertical line. If the graph intersects the line in more than one place at any interval, the graph does not represent a function.

Volume: The measure of the three-dimensional space a solid object fills.

x-axis: The horizontal axis of the Cartesian grid.

x-coordinate: Part of the definition of a point; the first coordinate of a coordinate pair and the location of the point as it relates to the x-axis.

x-intercept: The point on a line at which it intercepts the x-axis, which is also the point at which the y-coordinate equals 0.

y-axis: The vertical axis of the Cartesian grid.

y-coordinate. Part of the definition of a point; the second coordinate of a coordinate pair and the location of the point as it relates to the y-axis.

y-intercept: The point on a line at which it intercepts the y-axis, which is also the point at which the x-coordinate equals 0.

Standardized Tests and High School Math

Before you use this to prepare for whatever test looms before you, be aware that the way to excel on these tests is not, generally, to learn the math. Standardized tests measure your test-taking smarts more than your actual knowledge, so you are better off learning those skills from the appropriate Princeton Review book. When in doubt, the best way to a problem is the easiest way (but it's nice to know the reason it all works, too). So, onwards!

MATH LEVEL I SAT II

Chapter 1 Algebraic Expressions page 1, chapter 2 Solving Algebraic Equations page 15, chapter 3 Exponents and Roots page 31, chapter 4 Logarithms page 43, chapter 5 Polynomials page 49, chapter 6 Inequalities page 73, chapter 7 Permutations, Combinations, and the Binomial Theorem page 77, chapter 8 Plane Geometry page 87, chapter 9 Solid Geometry page 123, chapter 10 Analytic Geometry page 131, chapter 11 Parabolas page 151, chapter 12 Other Conics page 173, chapter 13 Trigonometry of Degrees page 187, chapter 14 Trigonometry of Radians page 207.

MATH LEVEL II SAT II

Chapter 1 Algebraic expressions page 1, chapter 2 Solving Algebraic Equations page 15, chapter 3 Exponents and Roots page 31, chapter 4 Logarithms page 43, chapter 5 Polynomials page 49, chapter 6 Inequalities page 73, chapter 7 Permutations, Combinations, and the Binomial Theorem page 77, chapter 8 Plane Geometry page 87, chapter 9 Solid Geometry page 123, chapter 10 Analytic Geometry page 131, chapter 11 Parabolas page 151, chapter 12 Other Conics page 173, chapter 13 Trigonometry of Degrees page 187, chapter 14 Trigonometry of Radians page 207.

SAT MATH SECTION

Chapter 1 Algebraic expressions page 1, chapter 2 Solving Algebraic Equations page 15, chapter 3 Exponents and Roots page 31, Parts of chapter 5 Polynomials page 49, chapter 6 Inequalities page 73, chapter 8 Plane Geometry page 87, chapter 9 Solid Geometry: only volume and surface area, chapter 10 Analytic Geometry: only plotting points and lines, and slope.

GRE MATH SECTION

Chapter 1 Algebraic expressions page 1, chapter 2 Solving Algebraic Equations page 15, chapter 3 Exponents and Roots page 31, Parts of chapter 5 Polynomials page 49, chapter 6 Inequalities page 73, chapter 8 Plane Geometry page 87, chapter 9 Solid Geometry: only volume and surface area.

GMAT Math Section: Chapter 1 Algebraic expressions page 1, chapter 2 Solving Algebraic Equations page 15, chapter 3 Exponents and Roots page 31, Parts of chapter 5 Polynomials page 49, chapter 6 Inequalities page 73, chapter 8 Plane Geometry page 87, chapter 9 Solid Geometry: only volume and surface area.

ACT

Chapter 1 Algebraic expressions page 1, chapter 2 Solving Algebraic Equations page 15, chapter 3 Exponents and Roots page 31, chapter 5 Polynomials page 49, chapter 6 Inequalities page 73, chapter 8 Plane Geometry page 87, chapter 9 Solid Geometry page 123, chapter 10 Analytic Geometry page 131, chapter 13 Trigonometry of Degrees page 187, chapter 14 Trigonometry of Radians page 207.

Trigonometric Identities

$$\text{sine or sin} = \frac{opp}{hyp}$$

$$\text{cosine or cos} = \frac{adj}{hyp}$$

$$\text{tangent or tan} = \frac{opp}{adj}$$

$$\text{cosecant or csc} = \frac{hyp}{adj}$$

$$\text{secant or sec} = \frac{hyp}{opp}$$

$$\text{cotangent or cot} = \frac{adj}{opp}$$

$$\text{cosecant or } \csc = \frac{1}{\sin}$$

$$\text{secant or } \sec = \frac{1}{\cos}$$

$$\text{cotangent or } \cot = \frac{1}{\tan}$$

$$\cot = \frac{\cos}{\sin}$$

$$\tan = \frac{\sin}{\cos}$$

$$\sin \theta = y$$

$$\cos \theta = x$$

$$\tan \theta = \frac{y}{x}$$

$$\csc \theta = \frac{1}{y}$$

$$\sec \theta = \frac{1}{x}$$

$$\cot \theta = \frac{x}{y}$$

$$\sin -\theta = -\sin \theta$$

$$\cos -\theta = \cos \theta$$

$$\tan -\theta = -\tan \theta$$

$$\csc -\theta = -\csc \theta$$

$$\sec -\theta = \sec \theta$$

$$\cot -\theta = -\cot \theta$$

$$\sin^2 \theta + \cos^2 \theta = 1$$

$$\tan^2 \theta + 1 = \sec^2 \theta$$

$$1 + \cot^2 \theta = \csc^2 \theta$$

The addition formulas: For any two angles θ and ϕ, their functions are combined as follows.

$$\sin (\theta + \phi) = \sin \theta \cos \phi + \cos \theta \sin \phi$$

$$\cos (\theta + \phi) = \cos \theta \cos \phi - \sin \theta \sin \phi$$

$$\tan (\theta + \phi) = \frac{\tan \theta + \tan \phi}{1 - \tan \theta \tan \phi}$$

THE SUBTRACTION LAWS:

$$\sin (\theta - \phi) = \sin \theta \cos - \cos \theta \sin$$

$$\cos (\theta - \phi) = \cos \cos - \sin \sin$$

$$\tan (\theta - \phi) = \frac{\tan \theta + \tan \phi}{1 - \tan \theta \tan \phi}$$

DOUBLE-ANGLE FORMULAS

$\sin 2\theta = 2 \sin\theta \cos\theta$

$\cos 2\theta = \cos^2\theta - \sin^2\theta$

$\tan 2\theta = \dfrac{2\tan\theta}{1 - \tan^2\theta}$

HALF-ANGLE FORMULAS

$2\cos^2\theta = 1 + \cos 2\theta$

$2\sin^2\theta = 1 - \cos 2\theta$

$2\tan\ \theta = 2\left(\dfrac{1 - \cos\theta}{\sin\theta}\right)$

LAW OF SINES

For any triangle ABC $\dfrac{\sin A}{a} = \dfrac{\sin B}{b} = \dfrac{\sin C}{c}$

LAW OF COSINES

For any triangle ABC, $c^2 = a^2 + b^2 - 2ab \cos C$, $a^2 = b^2 + c^2 - 2bc \cos A$, and $b^2 = a^2 + c^2 - 2ac \cos B$.

NOTES

NOTES

NOTES

NOTES

NOTES

NOTES

NOTES

ABOUT THE AUTHOR

Marcia Lerner graduated from Brown University in 1986. She has been teaching and writing for the Princeton Review since 1988. She lives in Brooklyn, N.Y.

More **Bestselling**
Smart Titles Available
from ➤ THE PRINCETON REVIEW